WHO IS RIGOBERTA M

GREG GRANDIN

VERSO

London • New York

This edition first published by Verso 2011
© Greg Grandin 2011
Chapter 1 originally appeared in *The American Historical Review*, Vol. 110,
Issue 1; Chapter 2 originally appeared in *The Specter of Genocide: Mass Murder
in Historical Perspective* (New York: Cambridge University Press, 2003)

The moral rights of the author have been asserted

1 3 5 7 9 10 8 6 4 2

Verso
UK: 6 Meard Street, London W1F 0EG
US: 20 Jay Street, Suite 1010, Brooklyn, NY 11201
www.versobooks.com

Verso is the imprint of New Left Books

ISBN-13: 978-1-84467-452-7 (hbk)
ISBN-13: 978-1-84467-458-9 (pbk)

British Library Cataloguing in Publication Data
A catalogue record for this book is available from the British Library

Library of Congress Cataloging-in-Publication Data
A catalog record for this book is available from the Library of Congress

Typeset in Minion by Hewer Text UK Ltd, Edinburgh
Printed in the US by Maple Vail

Contents

Preface

I reread *I, Rigoberta Menchú* last year, after Verso asked me to write an introduction for a new edition, having not taught or turned to the book for quite awhile. The controversy that had engulfed the memoir in the late 1990s, which included charges that Menchú misrepresented some aspects of her life, had increased the class time needed to teach it and there were other good, quick illustrations of Cold War terror in Central America one could assign, such as Marc Danner's *Massacre at El Mozote*, for instance. The intensity of the accusations and questions asked about Menchú's story—What was true? What wasn't? Who wrote it? Who, really, was Rigoberta Menchú and what did she want?—seems specific to the fixations of a time that was, in the US at least, more innocent: the last skirmish in the pre-9/11 culture wars. Today, students and scholars who have time to work through the always vexed relationship between history and memory continue to find the book useful. But the tribunes of culture and opinion can breezily dismiss it as a hoax, or as an example of "social or political witness stories that turns out to be works of fiction," as the *New Yorker* recently did, along with James Frey's discredited *A Million Little Pieces*. This is regrettable, for subsequent research—by individual scholars (see the suggestions for further reading) as well as sprawling, multi-year investigations by two truth commissions, one run by the Catholic Church and the other by the United Nations—has largely vindicated Menchú's version of events.

When I returned to the book, I half expected to find in

Menchú a left-wing John Galt, a character with no inner life, a pure propagandist. That's not the case. Throughout the narrative, but especially toward its end as Menchú moves toward exile and retrospection, her testimony reveals dissonant impulses, pleasure in the middle of terror and currents of despair running under surface triumphalism. Menchú, a semi-literate twenty-three-year-old with a few years of basic education, one of the few survivors of a slaughtered peasant family, conjures a battleground where her political battles seem almost slight compared to her own psychic ones. Listen to the recordings of the interviews that led to the book, done in Paris in 1982—they are available at the Hoover Institution Archives, in Stanford, California—and you will hear a disembodied tumble of words made substantial by anger and defiance, muted, perhaps numbed, by repetition, from having already told her story so many times to sympathizers, strangers, and reporters in an effort to raise awareness about what was happening in Guatemala. In one interview she did in the Montparnasse apartment of Arturo Taracena, a member of the insurgent Ejército Guerrillero de los Pobres (EGP) then working on his doctorate in history, Menchú recounts what she called *la vida mala* of peasants: "we are machines of production ... always producing, never receiving." "This isn't just my pain," she says, with the bells of the Église Saint-Pierre-de-Montrouge tolling faintly in the background, "but the pain of a whole people."

The introduction I wrote was not published in the new edition. Neither I nor Verso were aware that Elisabeth Burgos-Debray, the anthropologist and journalist who conducted most of the interview with Menchú, had the power, based on the original 1982 contract she signed with the French publisher, Éditions Gallimard, to approve or reject future editions and additional material that might be added to the English version of the book published by Verso. It is public knowledge that Burgos and Menchú, since the early 1990s, have been on bad terms and that in September 1993 Burgos asked Gallimard to stop sending Menchú her share of the royalties. Burgos told David Stoll, the US anthropologist who spent nearly a decade researching the veracity of Menchú's memoir, that the reason she did so was because the two women began to diverge politically over her criticism of Cuba, an account Burgos repeats in her preface to a second edition of Stoll's *Rigoberta Menchú and the Story of All Poor Guatemalans*, the book that led to Menchú's discrediting. Stoll, though, notes a second reason: around this time Menchú began to question the fact that she was not considered the book's legal author. "What is effectively a gap in the book is the question of the right of the author, right?" Menchú remarked in a 1991 interview. "Because the authorship of the book really should be more precise, shared, right?" Then in February 1993, Menchú asked Burgos to sign over the author's rights, "so that she could make her own contracts." This request was denied, and Stoll, whose book Burgos strongly endorses in her preface, suggests that Burgos "stopped the remittances" because of Menchú's complaints.[1]

All of the above occurred in the early 1990s, a full half decade before Stoll's exposé kicked off a firestorm of criticism against Menchú. In all of the ink spilt about that controversy, all of the accusations leveled against Menchú, not one

---

1. Stoll writes that Burgos "had always sent Rigoberta the *full* royalties," and reproduces in his book receipts showing that Menchú received 295,802 francs, about $59,000, between 1983 and 1993 (my emphasis). See David Stoll, *Rigoberta Menchú and the Story of All Poor Guatemalans* (Boulder, CO, 2008), 321. A Gallimard representative, however, told me that according to company records, until 1993, the company "paid [Menchú], upon request of Elisabeth Burgos, every year *part* of Burgos's royalties."

reporter, as far as I know, thought it worth mentioning that the book, whatever its intellectual and political provenance, did not legally belong to Menchú. I'm not especially politically correct, and have always thought that defenses of Menchú's memoir based on her position—that is, as an indigenous woman with claims to ways of knowing or speaking distinct from colonial knowledge—came up short. Yet this particular arrangement, whereby Menchú got the opprobrium but not the royalties her book generated, does seem unjust. And it perhaps accounts for her conflictive relationship to her own memoir. Faced with unrelenting, and often unfounded, criticism—discussed in more detail in the essay that follows—and cut off from its proceeds, Menchú has distanced herself from the book. She has moved on, continuing her work on the international stage as an advocate of indigenous rights and trying to launch a political career in Guatemala.

This is a shame, for the integrity of the memoir, both as a political and historical document, remains intact. Stoll has repeatedly justified his exposé by arguing that the popularity of *I, Rigoberta Menchú* built support *outside* of Guatemala that the insurgents had lost *inside* of the country, prolonging a war that would have ended much earlier, which only brought more misery to the "people," in whose name the guerrillas fought. This is simplistic and wrong. The political success of the book, its unexpected wild popularity in Europe and the US, actually strengthened the non-militarist wing of the insurgents, which was able to use the attention the book focused on Guatemala to create a political space that allowed for a negotiated end to the country's prolonged civil war. *I, Rigoberta Menchú*, with its forceful promotion of indigenous identity and rights, can in many ways be considered a precursor to the formation of guerrilla-allied organizations, such as GAM and CERJ (respectively, in English, the Mutual Support Group of Relatives of the

Disappeared and the Council of Ethnic Communities), which advocated on behalf of human rights and the rule of law in order to strengthen democratic institutions and compel the state and the military to the bargaining table.

And breezy repudiations by New York's literati notwithstanding, Menchú's work of course is not fiction. Hence this volume, which includes the introduction and also, for the first time in translation, the historical section of the United Nations–administered truth commission, the Comisión para el Esclarecimiento Histórico (CEH), or, in English, the Historical Clarification Commission. Published in June 1999, the CEH's twelve-volume final report fully confirms Menchú's interpretation of the conflict that took the lives of her brother, father, and mother. I, along with about 300 others, had worked with the commission, though had departed before its conclusions were drafted. One of the issues that dominated the commission—staffed largely by lawyers and other human rights professionals who work the international crisis circuit, from Haiti to Kosovo, with little specific knowledge of Guatemalan history or commitment to any particular interpretation of the war—was whether or not genocide against Mayan Indians had taken place. The assault on Mayan communities—over a hundred thousand dead, hundreds of villages, including Menchú's, razed—was undeniable. But the debate was: Did the military and its allies kill Mayans because they were Mayan or because they were the real or imagined support base of the insurgents?

To answer this question, the CEH did what no other truth commission had done before or has done since: it gave a team of Guatemalan historians and social scientists (composed of intellectuals from across the political spectrum, absent the recalcitrant right) access to its research—including an enormous database of over eight thousand testimonies, about a dozen "context reports," or local histories, composed by the CEH's regional offices, interviews with key actors, including former presidents, military strategists, death squad members, and guerrilla leaders, thousands of declassified US government documents, and an extensive library of secondary sources—and asked them to write an analysis of the "causes" and "origins" of the human rights abuses. The result was a sweeping interpretation of Guatemalan history that went well beyond the often vacuous "reconciliation talk" of past truth commissions. Also included in this volume are two essays discussing the Guatemalan truth commission's precedent-setting use of historical analysis and its genocide ruling.

Ultimately, what was at stake in the Menchú controversy was a question of responsibility; those who seized on her disputed testimony argued that Guatemalan political repression was largely a contingent reaction to New Left guerrilla provocation— thus holding revolutionaries such as Menchú and her father answerable for the onslaught. But the CEH, based on extensive and diverse sources, unambiguously concluded that the war was "historically and structurally determined," tracing how colonial racism, exploitation, and authoritarianism evolved to the point where genocide and counterinsurgency became indistinguishable social projects. The Guatemalan commission did not say, as the South African truth commission did, that armed struggle was morally justified—a claim that Menchú was heavily criticized for. Yet it did unequivocally understand the guerrillas as emerging from a society that allowed no possibility for peaceful reform: "Social injustice led to protest and subsequently to political instability, to which there were always only two responses: repression or military coups. Confronted by movements calling for economic, political, social, or cultural change, the state increasingly resorted to terror in order to maintain social control. Political violence was thus a direct expression of structural violence . . ."

Let me end this already too long preface to what was meant

to be an introduction with words from a Nobel Prize winner—
not Rigoberta Menchú, who received the honor in 1992, but
Aleksandr Solzhenitsyn, who was awarded the prize for literature in 1971. In the great fallout that resulted from the defeat of
the global New Left, followed shortly by the collapse of Soviet
Communism, these two laureates occupy exact opposite ends
of the debate over the meaning of the twentieth century. The
dissemination of Solzhenitsyn's work, first in Europe and then
in the United States, exposed the Soviet system as bankrupt and,
for many, the "gulag" as the terminus, metaphorically or actually, of the Marxist tradition. In contrast, Menchú, during the
early years of her fame, was taken up by those who refused to see
in the failure of the USSR an absolute indictment of all militant
social movements and who insisted that the historical injustices
of colonialism, along with the violence involved in maintaining
first world domination of the third, was as urgent an issue as
human rights in Russia. Then, in the late 1990s, when accusations called Menchú's testimony into question, those most likely
to demonize Menchú, or dismiss her as a dupe, were also likely
to celebrate Solzhenitsyn as a moral beacon. Solzhenitsyn's
most famous work of course is *The Gulag Archipelago*, a book of
irreproachable esteem, described upon its publication as "non-
fiction" (*Washington Post*), depicting "only true facts," a "factual
documentary" (*New York Times*), and, by Solzhenitsyn himself,
as containing "no fictional persons, nor fictional events ... all
took place just as it is here described." But the respected Russian
historian Roy Medvedev, as part of a broader study of Stalinism,
writes that Solzhenitsyn "distorted many details" in that book
and that he did so for political reasons.[2]

2. Roy Aleksandrovich Medvedev, *Let History Judge: The Origins and Consequences of Stalinism*, translated by George Shriver (New York, 1989), 273.

No one, rightly, would use such distortions either to diminish the horrors of the gulag or to present a sweeping reinterpretation of Stalinism, as Menchú's critics do for Cold War terror in Latin America. As far as I know, no major publication felt compelled to follow up Medvedev's findings with a full-on inquisition into every nook of Solzhenitsyn's life, into every unverifiable statement he ever made, along the lines of the frenzy unleashed on Menchú. This dispensation extends not just to the content of Solzhenitsyn's book but its style. Human rights intellectuals, such as the French philosopher Bernard-Henri Lévy, insisted that what separated Solzhenitsyn's "experiment in literary investigation" (as the author described his method) from dry statistical or fact-based accounts of Soviet terror was its ability to invoke "that aspect of myth, of fiction, of the symbolic that makes it possible that Evil, which cannot be thought, can be represented."[3] Menchú of course was pilloried for doing just that. "The criminal oppression of indigenous peoples in Guatemala cannot be disputed," wrote the New York Times, after one of its reporters scoured the Guatemalan highlands to find evidence contradicting Menchú's memoir. "Why, then," the Times editorial asked, "the sinking feeling upon learning that some of the essential facts in 'I, Rigoberta Menchu' are not true? In a war between unequals, especially when the more powerful side is rampantly duplicitous, we expect that truth will be on the side of the innocent."

Perhaps. But who gets to carry the heavy weight of "innocence" is itself a consequence of the "war between unequals." This study in contrast, this double standard, in how the work of the learned Solzhenitsyn and the unlettered Menchú has

---

3. In Kristin Ross, *May '68 and Its Afterlives* (Chicago, 2002), 171.

been incorporated into the West's moral education speaks volumes about the meaning and legacy of racism and the Cold War, providing one more reason why Menchú's testimony, in addition to its intrinsic power, should still be taught and valued. As Solzhenitsyn said in his 1971 Nobel lecture, the worth of literature and language is their ability to pass from generation to generation an "irrefutable condensed experience," a "living memory" that must remain "safe from deformation and slander."

Greg Grandin
New York City
October 2010

Introduction: A Victory Described in Detail

Dante's Inferno "is out"; *I, Rigoberta Menchú* "is in," the *Wall Street Journal* wrote, in late 1988, of Stanford University's decision to include Third World authors in its required curriculum. "Virgil, Cicero and Tacitus give way to Frantz Fanon," the paper said, concerned that Stanford's new reading list viewed "the West" not through the "evolution of such ideas as faith and justice, but through the prism of sexism, racism and the faults of its ruling class." Herewith began the metamorphosis of a young and relatively obscure Guatemalan Mayan woman into something considerably more than a witness to genocide.

Since its publication in English in 1984, Rigoberta Menchú Tum's memoir had been assigned with increasing frequency in university courses in the US and Europe. Historians taught it as a primary source documenting revolution and repression in Guatemala and elsewhere in Latin America, anthropologists as first-person ethnography, and literary theorists as an example of *testimonio*, a genre distinct from traditional forms of autobiography. But Menchú's mention in the *Journal* thrust her further into the then escalating cultural wars, with conservatives holding her up as an example of the foibles of the multicultural Left. "Undergraduates do not read about Rigoberta," wrote the American Enterprise Institute's Dinesh D'Souza in 1991, "because she has written a great and immortal book, or performed a great deed, or invented something useful. She simply happened to be in the right place and the right time."

The place was Guatemala's Western Highlands, inhabited by some four million people, the majority poor indigenous peasants living in remote, hardscrabble villages like Chimel, Menchú's hometown. The time was the late 1970s, when the Guatemalan military was bringing to a climax a pacification campaign, the horror of which was matched only by historical memories of the Spanish conquest. By the time it was over, government forces had taken the lives of Menchú's parents, her two brothers, and two hundred thousand other Guatemalans. And though this campaign may have been "unfortunate for her personal happiness," D'Souza said, it was "indispensable for her academic reputation," transforming Menchú into a fetish object onto which "minority students" could affirm their "victim status" and professors could project their "Marxist and feminist views onto South American Indian culture."

Then in 1992, on the five-hundredth anniversary of Christopher Columbus's voyage to the Americas, Menchú won the Nobel Peace Prize, and whatever ability she had up until that point in maintaining the integrity of her particular story gave way to the burdens of representing the victims of imperialism everywhere. She was given the prize, the Nobel selection committee noted, not just for her work exposing the murder and mayhem committed by US allies in Guatemala but for serving as a "vivid symbol of peace and reconciliation" in a world still scarred by European colonialism.

It is safe to say that most who read her book did not interpret her tale as "an explicit indictment of the historical role of the West or Western institutions," as D'Souza feared, but rather as a saga of individual resilience in the face of great hardship, much like Anne Frank's diary. If anything, Menchú held out the possibility of redemption, as the Nobel committee suggested. Unlike Anne Frank, she survived. And following the end of the Cold War, many intellectuals and policy makers hoping to construct a *pax neoliberal* were willing to acknowledge that victory over the Soviet Union had entailed some moral compromises. Support of "widespread repression" was "wrong," said US President Bill Clinton, a "mistake" that the "United States must not repeat."

Yet, as far as irreconcilables on the cultural and political Right were concerned, the Peace Prize might as well have been given posthumously to Frantz Fanon or Che Guevara. Trapped as they are by the fallacy of a consequent logic, where to admit A would mean accepting Z, those most hostile to Menchú believed that to acknowledge her legitimacy would indeed indict the whole of the West and all of its works. The attacks came fast after she won the Nobel Peace Prize, with detractors working hard to expose Menchú as an Indian with an agenda. They demanded that she "come clean" about her involvement with Guatemalan guerrillas, renounce her support of the Sandinistas in neighboring Nicaragua, and denounce human rights violations in Cuba. D'Souza thought it suspicious that Menchú met her "feminist translator"—Elisabeth Burgos, once married to Che's comrade Régis Debray—"in Paris, not a venue to which many of the Third World's poor routinely travel" and that her "rhetoric employs a socialist and Marxist vocabulary that does not sound typical of a Guatemalan peasant."

What truly irked though was not the language but the details. "No details! Never bother me with details!" pleads the archbishop in Jean-Paul Sartre's 1951 *The Devil and the Good Lord*, hoping to be spared the specifics of a violent military suppression of a peasant revolt. Sartre's sixteenth-century cleric knew what Cold War triumphalists feared: "a victory described in detail is indistinguishable from a defeat." And Menchú provided too many details.

Rigoberta Menchú Tum was twenty-three years old when she arrived in Paris in January 1982, where she gave the interview that would produce her memoir, and the worst of Guatemala's civil war was yet to come. The roots of the crisis reached back to five years before Menchú was born, to the CIA's 1954 overthrow of the democratically elected Jacobo Arbenz. The agency had objected to the fact Arbenz legalized a small communist party and implemented an extensive agrarian reform. Following the coup, Washington promised that it would turn Guatemala into a 'showcase for democracy." Instead, it created a laboratory of repression. After the costly Korean War, US policy makers decided that the best way to confront communism was not on the battlefield but by strengthening the "internal defense" of allied countries. Guatemala, now ruled by a pliant and venal regime, proved a perfect test case, as Washington supplied a steadily increasing infusion of military aid and training. US diplomats often signaled a desire to work with a "democratic Left"—that is, a non-communist Left. But the most passionate defenders of democracy were likely to be found in the ranks of Washington's opponents and singled out for execution by US-created and funded security forces.

By the late 1970s, more than two decades after the overthrow of Arbenz, the Guatemalan government stood on the point of collapse. Repression against reformist politicians, a radicalized Catholic Church, indigenous activists, and a revived labor and peasant movement swelled the ranks of a left-wing insurgency that, by the end of the decade, was operating in eighteen of Guatemala's twenty-two departments. Between 1976 and 1980, security forces killed or disappeared close to a thousand Social and Christian Democrats, trade unionists, university professors and students. By 1980, death squads were running rampant in Guatemala City and the countryside, and mutilated bodies piled up on the streets and in ravines.

In the indigenous highlands, violence against activists had been commonplace since the 1954 overthrow of Arbenz, and steadily increased through the 1960s and 1970s. Menchú's brother, Petrocinio, was murdered in late 1979. Repression of Catholic priests and catechists reached such a pitch that the Church shuttered its diocese in the department of El Quiché in 1980, and the first of many assaults on Menchú's village took place that year on Christmas Eve. The massacres started in 1981, and at first were not linked to a plan of stabilization or rule. Then in March 1982, shortly after Menchú's Paris interview, a military coup in Guatemala brought an even more vicious, yet more competent, regime to power. In an effort to eliminate the insurgent threat without generating wider circles of radicalization, military analysts marked Mayan communities according to colors: *white* spared those thought to have no rebel influence; *pink* identified areas in which the insurgency had a limited presence—suspected guerrillas and their supporters were to be killed but the communities left standing; *red* gave no quarter—all were to be executed and villages destroyed. "One of the first things we did," said an architect of this plan, "was draw up a document for the campaign with annexes and appendices. It was a complete job with planning down to the last detail."[1]

A subsequent investigation by the United Nations Comisión para el Esclarecimiento Histórico (CEH)—a truth commission—called this genocide. The CEH documented a total of 626 army massacres, most of which took place between early 1982 and 1983—that is, the period between Menchú's interview and her book's publication in French and Spanish. In a majority of cases, the commission found

> evidence of multiple ferocious acts preceding, accompanying, and following the killing of the victims. The assassination of children,

---

1. Jennifer Schirmer, *The Guatemalan Military Project: A Violence Called Democracy* (Philadelphia, 2000), 44–9.

often by beating them against the wall or by throwing them alive
into graves to be later crushed by the bodies of dead adults; amputation of limbs; impaling victims; pouring gasoline on people and
burning them alive; extraction of organs; removal of fetuses from
pregnant women ... The military destroyed ceremonial sites, sacred
places, and cultural symbols. Indigenous language and dress were
repressed ... Legitimate authority of the communities was destroyed.

Massacres broke the agricultural cycle, leading to hunger
and widespread deprivation as refugees hiding in the mountains and lowland jungle scavenged roots and wild plants to
survive. A million and a half people, up to 80 percent of the
population in some areas, were driven from their homes, with
entire villages left abandoned.

This scorched-earth campaign was designed to cut off
indigenous communities from the insurgency and break
down the communal structures which military analysts identified as the seedbed of guerrilla support. This explains the
exceptionally savage nature of the counterinsurgency, which,
while comprising the most centralized and rationalized phase
of the war, was executed on the ground with a racist frenzy.
The point was not just to eliminate the guerrillas and their
real and potential supporters but to colonize the indigenous
spaces, symbols, and social relations military strategists
believed to be outside of state control. Terror was made spec-
tacle. Soldiers and their paramilitary allies raped women in
front of husbands and children. Security forces singled out
religious activists for murder and turned churches into torture
chambers. "They say that that the soldiers scorched earth,"
one survivor told me, "but it was heaven that they burned."

I, Rigoberta Menchú cut through the shroud that surrounded
this slaughter, revealing a hidden history of pain and death.
The heartbreaking murders of Menchú's brother, father, and

mother mark key turning points in a powerful coming-of-age story, where the protagonist's progress as a politically aware person merges with the revolutionary momentum of society as a whole. Menchú presents her father's long struggle to defend their village's land against the predations of planters as typical of the dispossession suffered by Guatemala's peasants, and subtly melds indigenous rituals and beliefs to the ideals of liberation theology, a current in Catholicism that sought to align itself with the poor. Having given her interview prior to the genocide that turned the tide of the war in favor of the military, Menchú brings readers to the edge of the abyss. We now know that the revolution was doomed to fail, and there are hints throughout her book that Menchú knew it as well. By her story's end, she lingers timorously on the cusp of the looming apocalypse, which she tries to forestall by increasingly asserting the inevitability of the people's victory.

In one passage, Menchú recalls hiding in the capital before her flight to Mexico, sick with ulcers, unable to rise from bed for days at a time, finding consolation that she "wasn't the only orphan in Guatemala" and that her grief was the "grief of a whole people." For a moment, she is bearing the burdens of "all poor Guatemalans" not to predict triumph but to accept loss. Having unexpectedly reunited with her twelve-year-old sister, Menchú demands to know what kind of world is it that could produce such misery: "How is it possible for our parents to be no longer with us?" Her anguish leads her to fantasize about succumbing to some unnamed "vice," a "depravity," so that she would no longer "have to think or bear life." Menchú would go on to escape Guatemala and achieve international recognition. Here though she glimpses the oblivion that was the fate of some war widows and orphans. The vices available to Mayan women were sex and drink, and starting in the late 1970s, indigenous prostitutes, refugees from decimated families, began to haunt the margins of Guatemala City's downtown, many still dressed in native *traje*. A more common fortune was to struggle on in solitude, trying to hold what was left of one's family together. Menchú's despair, however, is fleeting. "What has happened is a sign of victory," she reports her sister telling her, "a revolutionary isn't born out of something good" but of "wretchedness and bitterness." Having confirmed her commitment to the struggle, this triumphalism is obviously less propaganda than deflection, a way to put off reckoning with incalculable loss and barely controlled rage. "We have to fight without measuring our suffering," she recalls her sister telling her.

In 1999, David Stoll, a professor of anthropology at Middlebury College who had spent nearly a decade researching the veracity of Menchú's story, published his findings, charging that the Nobel Laureate exaggerated and otherwise distorted some of the events chronicled in her autobiography. Many who knew Guatemala well thought Stoll's book, *Rigoberta Menchú and the Story of All Poor Guatemalans,* a strange exercise in compulsion, in which the author repeatedly reaffirmed his admiration for Menchú but then drove himself to dispute even her off-handed comments. "What rankles," wrote journalist and novelist Francisco Goldman—who himself has spent many years peeling back the layers of the baroque conspiracy surrounding the 1998 execution of Guatemalan bishop Juan José Gerardi—"is the whiff of ideological obsession and zealotry, the odor of unfairness and meanness, the making of a mountain out of a molehill."

Two of Stoll's charges concerning Menchú's life do have merit. First, he documents that she received some education, contradicting a claim that her father refused to send her to school because he did not want her to lose her cultural identity. Second, Stoll presents evidence that Menchú falsely placed herself at the scene of her sixteen-year-old brother's murder. Petrocinio Menchú was kidnapped by the military when his sister said he was, and along with other captives brought to the town of Chajul, accused of being a guerrilla and murdered to intimidate the population. Menchú's account of the execution, Stoll believes, "can be considered factual." Except that she, most likely, did not witness it firsthand. As to Menchú's equally harrowing description of her mother's killing, Stoll grants that "Rigoberta's account is basically true".[2]

The *New York Times* highlighted Stoll's accusations in an above-the-fold, front-page story, while journals high and low—the *New Republic*, the *New York Review of Books*, *Time* magazine, the *New York Post*—weighed in.[3] Some took the opportunity to pen lengthy meditations on the relationship of facts to memory in a preliterate, traumatized peasant society. Others simply swiped at the academic Left, lumping Menchú with Edward Said, whose autobiography was just then also coming under attack for allegedly obscuring some facts of his life while embroidering others. Conservatives, of course, seized on Stoll's accusations. David Horowitz called *I, Rigoberta Menchú* "a tissue of lies" and "one of the greatest hoaxes of the 20th century . . . virtually everything that Menchú has written is a lie." He took out ads in college papers, condemning Menchú as a "Marxist-terrorist," denouncing professors who continued to teach her book, and calling for the revocation of her Peace Prize.

---

2. *Rigoberta Menchú and the Story of all Poor Guatemalans*, 127.

3. It is often wrongly believed that Stoll accuses Menchú of fabricating the story that her brother Nicolás died of starvation. That charge in fact comes from the *New York Times* article, which writes that a "younger brother whom Ms. Menchú says she saw die of starvation never existed." This is false. Menchú did have a brother named Nicolás who died of hunger.

For his part, Stoll seemed caught off guard by a controversy that was quickly escaping his control, offering contradictory statements to explain the point of his research. His book dedicated a chapter to proving that Menchú could not have witnessed her brother's execution, yet he now said that "how one member or another of her family died" was a minor issue. Stoll confirmed the "essential factuality of Menchú's account of how her brother and mother died," yet complained to a reporter that she was "still displaying a lack of candor" in answering his charges. He distanced himself from the Right, defending Menchú's status as a Nobel Laureate, and flailed at the Left, complaining that members of the "Menchú cult" had called him "everything but an infidel Jew."[4]

---

4. Stoll often complained, at the height of the dispute, that Menchú's defenders accused him of being a CIA agent. I never met anyone who believed this, and always thought that the charge, if it was in fact made, grants him too much coherence. He did, though, appear to me to be another familiar US type, an innocent abroad fumbling through the wreckage of Guatemalan history, offering little more than a derivative on what is now a long established critique, discussed below, of revolutionary politics dating back at least to the French Revolution. Prevented by an historical illiteracy from fully claiming this intellectual tradition and realizing his argument, Stoll digs deeper, insisting that the narrative inconsistencies of a twenty-three-year-old semi-literate war orphan hold the key to knowledge. Over time, his sense of persecution has only deepened. In a new Afterword to the second, 2008, edition of his *Rigoberta Menchú and the Story of All Poor Guatemalans,* he begins to refer to himself in the third person, less like Jorge Luis Borges than George on Seinfeld, attributing the career stall of "David Stoll" to shadowy conspiratorial forces subordinated to the "magical powers of those six syllables, Rigoberta Menchú" (297). Stoll's obsession with Menchú is here fully displayed; he assails her for

Stoll himself had criticized the "postmodern scholarship" of Edward Said in his book, yet now he pleaded with those gripped by the scandal to keep focused on Guatemala. His point was not to discredit Menchú, he said. He rather wanted to contest popular and scholarly explanations of Guatemala's civil war that presented the insurgent Ejército Guerrillero de los Pobres (EGP) and its peasant and Christian affiliates—such as those extolled by Menchú—as growing out of a collective experience of historic racism and economic exploitation. Instead, Stoll argues that conditions in the Western Highlands were improving for most indigenous peasants in the 1970s and that the state had conducted widespread political repression not to uphold an unjust system but merely "to get at" the EGP, which was largely led by middle-class urban radicals with little connection to or support in the peasant communities they presumed to liberate. It was the guerrillas, therefore, that pre-empted the possibility of peaceful reform by bringing to power the "homicidal wing" of the military. Mayans, for their part, joined the rebels in droves only to escape state terror, not because social conditions drove them—or ideals motivated them—to make a revolution.

To make his case, Stoll actually focuses less on Rigoberta Menchú than on her father, Vicente, presenting him as a

---

speaking at US colleges and offering little but ecological- and indigenous-rights platitudes: "Rigoberta is intelligent, she has a salty peasant humor, and she could tell Americans a lot more" (as if when Thomas Friedman or Bill Clinton collect enormous speaking fees for college speeches they customarily reveal what they know about how the world really works). In particular, Stoll believes Menchú should be honest about how "peasants are multiplying their children out of any possibility of maintaining their traditional way of life" (299).

litigious landowner locked in a decades-long quarrel not with rich ladino planters, as his daughter described, but with his wife's family. In the years prior to his death, Vicente Menchú was evicted from his land, jailed, and beaten, Stoll confirms, but those primarily responsible for his torment were his Mayan in-laws, the Tums. He also guesses that Vicente Menchú was not as politically active and astute as his daughter made him out to be, notwithstanding his involvement in peasant leagues, local development projects, and the Catholic catechist movement. He speculates that Rigoberta Menchú, too, came to her "political consciousness" late, largely in reaction to the murders of her brother, father, and mother, and perhaps spent the time her family was being persecuted enjoying life at Catholic boarding schools. From these conjectures, Stoll makes what he considers his most important deduction: that the Menchús stumbled into their alliance with the insurgents, and they did so not because they were determined to overthrow an intolerable social system but because they hoped to gain the upper hand against their peasant rivals[5]. In so

---

5. This argument echoes, in stripped-down form, what scholars call "rational-choice counterinsurgent theory," in which the cause and outcome of social conflict is reduced to a single variable: coercion. "When two forces are contending for the loyalty of, and control over, the civilian populations," declared a 1962 essay in *Foreign Affairs*, "the side which uses violent reprisals most aggressively will dominate most of the people, even though their sympathies may lie in the other direction." As in rational-choice theory more broadly applied, individuals are abstracted from larger social and cultural relations (exactly the kind described in rich detail by Menchú) and presented as maximizing units weighing and acting on narrow individual interests (exactly how Stoll portrays Vicente Menchú). For its origins in Vietnam, see Ron Robin, *The Making of the Cold War Enemy: Culture and*

doing, they—and their neighbors—reaped the whirlwind.

Stoll complained that, amidst all the scandal's noise, the larger point of his research was getting drowned out. Only it was not. Right-wing activists, again, finely attuned to how A leads to Z, knew exactly what was at stake. They said it more shrilly, but they said more or less the same thing: "The fact is that there was no social ground for the armed insurrection that these Castroists tried to force," Horowitz wrote; ultimately "the source of the violence and ensuing misery that Rigoberta Menchú describes in her destructive little book is the left itself."

Conservatives recognized the value of Stoll's argument because it had been made before, at least as early as 1790, when Edmund Burke said France's old regime was in the process of self-reformation before ideologues who read too much Rousseau derailed things. In fact, Stoll's position parallels, probably unwittingly, more recent revisionist arguments concerning the French Revolution. Since feudalism was already on the wane prior to 1789, revolutionary militancy did not advance liberalization but rather represented a ghastly *dérapage,* as François Furet put it, a slide into chaos. In later work, Furet revised his opinion, rejecting the contingent implications of the word *dérapage* to argue that the "very idea of revolution" generated Jacobin terror. It is a position that runs to the core of contemporary debates concerning the causes of militancy, between those who see conflict as rooted in larger social relations, with violence resulting from the

---

Politics in the Military-Intellectual Complex (Princeton University Press, 2001). For its application in Central America starting in the mid 1960s, see Greg Grandin, *Empire's Workshop: Latin America, the United States, and the Rise of the New Imperialism* (New York, 2005), chapter 3.

instigating intransigence of elites, and those who blame terror on utopian ideological fervor. While the latter position has been used to explain events in Europe and the United States, such as the Holocaust, Stalinism, and the radical New Left, it holds considerably less influence in the Third World, where the relationship between repression, on the one hand, and colonialism, imperialism, and capitalism, on the other, is hard to deny.

Thus the broad resonance, beyond anything having to do with Guatemala, of the Menchú controversy. Guatemala has long been recognized as one of the most exploited societies in a region defined by exploitation, a place where many Mayans were subject to what was in effect slavery well into the twentieth century. The role of the United States in terminating the first and still so far only government that tried to democratize the country has been so well documented that it has become the mainstream example of choice when one wants to illustrate the misuse of Washington's power abroad. It even forced a sitting US president to apologize. The catastrophe that followed the 1954 coup had staggering human costs, resulting in one of the most savage wars in twentieth-century Latin America. So, if it could be demonstrated that political violence in northern Quiché—among the poorest of regions in the poorest of departments in the poorest of countries—was caused not by land dispossession, racism, or aborted reform but by, as Stoll thinks, "middle-class radicals" entranced by the Cuban Revolution, then the whole of Latin American history would be up for grabs. And, indeed, by the end of his book, Stoll has parlayed discrepancies in Menchú's story into a blanket indictment of the Latin American Left throughout its Cold War history, blaming the rise of death-squad dictatorships in

Chile, Argentina, and other countries in the 1970s on the "misguided belief in the moral purity of total rejection, of refusing to compromise with the system and seeking to overthrow it by force."

It is hard, though, to hang such a grand interpretation on the personal motives of one disputatious indigenous peasant and the imaginative license of his twenty-three-year-old orphaned exile. But Stoll does try, insisting on tracing nearly every act of aggression Menchú attributes to ladinos, planters or security forces back to an original provocation committed by her father. Nowhere is this shadow narrative more perversely applied than in his account of an event that serves as the climax of both Menchú's memoir and Stoll's riposte: the January 1980 firebombing of the Spanish embassy, which resulted in the death of Vicente Menchú and over thirty other peasants and university students who were protesting escalating military repression in the countryside, including the killing of Petrocinio Menchú. Investigations by the Spanish government, the Catholic Church, and the United Nations all confirmed Menchú's description of events, and in 2005 a Spanish judge issued an arrest warrant for a former Guatemalan interior minister accused of ordering the bombing. But as the signal event in the civil war, a naked display of unyielding power when many Guatemalans realized that no reform would be tolerated or petition considered, Stoll cannot help but weigh in. He speculates that the protesters might have intentionally killed themselves to reinforce "the left's cult of martyrdom." It's hard to overstate how extraordinary this statement is, especially coming from a researcher who bases his legitimacy on opposing fact-based, empirical argumentation against the deductions of a politicized Left. There is no tradition of tactical suicide among Guatemala leftists, and there is not one piece of evidence, not one witness, not even among those critical of the protesters, to support the possibility that the embassy massacre could have been a "revolutionary suicide that included murdering hostages and fellow protesters." But the logic of his argument, if not the facts of the case, compels Stoll to consider it, and in so doing he transforms Vicente Menchú from victim to victimizer.

Subsequent research over the last decade has proven Stoll's provocative thesis about Guatemala's civil war to be largely wrong, while confirming Menchú's interpretation of events.[6] The definitive refutation has come from the Comisión para el Esclarecimiento Histórico—the aforementioned UN truth commission—which released its findings in early 1999, shortly after the Menchú controversy broke. Based on over eight thousand interviews and extensive archival and regional research conducted by a team of over two hundred investigators, the CEH, like Stoll, understands the escalating civil war as emerging from the fault lines of local conflicts, including petty family grievances and parochial land conflicts, often among peasants and between indigenous communities. But it places its examination of any given clash within the broader context of a militarized plantation economy where non-indigenous elites fought to hold on to their monopoly control over land, labor, markets, credit, and transportation. As to Chimel, commission investigators recognized local feuds between peasants but also found evidence that ladino planters did play a crucial role in instigating violence and dispossession in the 1960s and '70s. On the key point of chronology, which is ultimately the hook on which Stoll's case dangles, the CEH documents a clear pattern of repression

---

6. See the appendix "Suggestions for Further Reading" for this scholarship.

enacted by planters, ladinos, and security forces in the indigenous highlands well before the arrival of the guerrillas in the 1970s. In the case of Chimel, Stoll says the army showed up only after the EGP guerrillas executed two ladinos in the spring of 1979, thus laying blame for the ensuing spiral of events that claimed the life of Menchú's brother and mother and the destruction of Chimel at the feet of her father's allies. But CEH researchers dated the beginning of the military's harassment of Chimel to earlier than this first EGP action.

The CEH is concerned less with identifying who fired the first shot in any one skirmish than with understanding the larger causes of the civil war. Starting with an introduction that provides staggering statistical evidence of inequality—Guatemala's health, education, literacy, and nutritional indicators continued to be among the most unjust in the world despite an abundance of natural wealth—the CEH's final report offers a damning analysis of Guatemalan history:

> From independence in 1821, an event led by the country's elite, an authoritarian state was created that excluded the majority of Guatemalans; it was racist in theory and practice and served to protect the interests of a small, privileged elite . . . State violence has been fundamentally aimed against the excluded, the poor, and the Maya, as well as those who struggled in favor of a just and more equitable society . . . Thus a vicious circle was created in which social injustice led to protest and subsequently to political instability, to which there were always only two responses: repression or military coups.

Confronted with movements demanding reform, the commission concluded, contrary to those who would blame the insurgency on Cuba or on the romance of revolution, the "state increasingly resorted to violence and terror in order to maintain social control. Political violence was thus a direct expression of structural violence."

To questions concerning her schooling and her brother's execution, Menchú has offered straightforward answers. In a 1999 interview, she said she omitted discussing her experience as a student and servant in the Colegio Belga because she hoped to protect the identities of the Catholic nuns who were involved in the kind of pastoral activism associated with liberation theology. "How I would have loved to tell of all the experiences I had," she said, but "the last thing I would have wanted during those years was to associate the Belgian school with me." Menchú did not study with the rest of the students, and only took classes part time a few days a week in the afternoon, working to pay for her room and board as a maid, cleaning the school in the morning and evening, earning twelve quetzals a month, about twelve dollars.[7] She admits she did not witness the murder of her

---

7. From the fact that Menchú did receive some education, Stoll extrapolates his other, conjectural, allegations: that she could not have worked on plantations as a child; could not have served as a maid; and could not have been involved in the kind of politics she narrates. But there is no reason why Menchú could not have labored on plantations either prior to leaving Chimel to attend school or during the yearly recess, which is timed to coincide with the coffee harvest. And Menchú's answer here suggests that her activism and her work as a servant was bound up with her education and her relationship with Catholic nuns, many of whom did play an important role in the consciousness-raising activities of the 1970s. Hal Cohen, in an essay otherwise sympathetic to Stoll, notes Stoll's strategy of citing the lack of evidence for many of Menchú's statements "as a symptom of a falsehood." "The Unmaking of Rigoberta Menchú", *Lingua Franca*, July–August 1999.

brother, but related an account of his killing, including the disputed fact that he was burned alive, from her mother. "And in response to whether my brothers, my father, were rich," she said to accusations that her family was relatively well-off, "go to Chimel and you will see for yourself."[8]

Menchú would not be the first partisan or literary notable to rearrange events in his or her life. Think of Benjamin Franklin and Mark Twain. The lies of Henry Kissinger, also a Nobel Peace Laureate, are legion, yet no publisher would feel the need to include a preface—such as this—setting them in their proper context before reissuing one of his many books. A more appropriate comparison would be Betty Friedan, author of *The Feminist Mystique,* who portrayed herself as an alienated, apolitical housewife when in fact she was a long-time activist who hailed from a family with deep roots in the Left labor movement. Few would consider using Friedan's narrative manipulations to cast doubt on the reality of the experience she was describing.

More than a decade after the scandal, what is notable about *I, Rigoberta Menchú* is not its exaggerations but its realism. Menchú had arrived in Paris emotionally brutalized, her feelings raw, her sense of urgency to tell a compelling story high. She spoke flawed Spanish and had come from a society in which most information was transmitted orally, where hearsay and rumor, not documented fact, prevailed. (Her memoir is filled with references to how paperwork was used to trick or entrap peasants, along with stories of endless days wasted by her father travelling to the capital to sign a succession of meaningless government forms. One passage in particular highlights the impotence of peasant patriarchy when set against

---

8. In Arturo Arias, ed., *The Rigoberta Menchú Controversy* (Minneapolis, 2001), 110–3, for the Menchú quotations.

state bureaucracy: Menchú recounts how, as a child, her father took her to the government land office, told her to remain absolutely still, and then took off his hat and bowed to a man sitting behind a typewriter. "That's something else I used to dream about—that typewriter," she recalled.) Added to this, she had just survived over a year of hiding in exile, a period that demanded self-censorship. At the same time, her experience speaking to reporters and solidarity delegations prior to her Paris interviews probably led her to realize the value audiences place on eyewitness accounts. The need to draw attention to Guatemala, which compared to neighboring Nicaragua and El Salvador was being ignored by the international press, must have tempted her to place herself at the scene of the many crimes she describes. Menchú did not know her interviews with Burgos would produce a book, much less an international bestseller. She had no experience with the publishing industry. And she certainly could not have imagined that every one of her statements would be subject to fine-tooth scrutiny. And yet her narrative hews closely to a truthful chronology, and even her most serious embellishment—that she witnessed her brother being burned to death—"can be considered factual," according to her principal fact-checker.

Scholars commonly discuss *I, Rigoberta Menchú* as reflecting the communal nature of Mayan society, where oral storytelling blurs the line between individual and group experience. Historians Christopher Lutz and George Lovell reach deep into the past to argue that sixteenth-century indigenous accounts of the Spanish conquest were often written in the collective voice, and that when Menchú, on the first page of her memoir, cautions that her memory is poor and that the story she is about to tell is "not only my life, it's also the testimony of my people," she means it literally. "I can't force them to understand," Menchú repeated in her 1999 interview.

"Everything, for me, that was the story of my community is also my own story. I did not come from the air."[9]

But over the last decade, as greater light has been thrown on the process that led to the publication of *I, Rigoberta Menchú*, its protagonist has emerged even more as a determined, distinctive individual. Elisabeth Burgos, then working toward a doctorate in ethnopsychiatry—a new discipline used to treat Paris's burgeoning immigrant population, many from France's former colonies—had wanted to interview, according to one account, a generic "Guatemalan Mayan woman," not Menchú in particular. And aside from supplying the testimony, Menchú was not involved in the transcription, editing, revising, or translation of the book.[10] Yet the two principals who did carry out those tasks— Burgos and Arturo Taracena Arriola, a Guatemalan historian and EGP representative in Paris—confirm that Menchú took control of the interview, speaking in a strong, certain voice. Though Taracena and Burgos suggested topics to be covered, they, Taracena reports, had to "rethink the outline" because Menchú's "narrative capacity" went "beyond what

---

9. Arias, *The Rigoberta Menchú Controversy*, 113.

10.   *I, Rigoberta Menchú* is Ann Wright's English translation of *Me llamo Rigoberta Menchú y así me nació la conciencia*, published in Spain by Editorial Argos Vergara in 1983, itself pared down and edited by Burgos and Taracena from a transcript of seventeen audio tapes. The tapes are available to researchers at the Hoover Institution Archives as part of the Elisabeth Burgos-Debray Papers. For the interview and editing process, see "Arturo Taracena Breaks His Silence" in Arias, ed., *The Rigoberta Menchú Controversy*. See Ann Wright, "The Interpretation of Translation, the Translation of Testimony: Mediation in the Books of Rigoberta Menchú," *In Other Words*, Autumn 2000, No. 15, 13–25, for a discussion of the translation process

we had originally conceived . . . there was a profound literary quality to Rigoberta Menchú's voice." The editors corrected Menchú's Spanish grammar and syntax, and arranged her account chronologically, but, Taracena remarks, the "book is a narration only by Rigoberta, with her own rhythm, with her own inventions, if there are any, with her own emotions."

Burgos withdrew during the interview process, applying her doctoral training in ethnopsychiatry to treat Menchú as a psychoanalyst would an analysand. That is, she gave Menchú time to talk. And considering her clandestine life in Guatemala and exile in Mexico, swinging between bouts of depression and episodes of intense political activity, Menchú needed it. "Everything was piling up together," she remembers of hiding in Guatemala City, "it was all on top of me." In bed for days at a time and refusing to eat, Menchú had few people to talk to. "With all the horrors that I had inside me," she says, "it would have been comforting for me to be able to talk to all the *compañeros,* or people who understood me, people who were sympathetic." But put to work as a servant in a house of nuns, her loneliness grew "worse, because as I washed the clothes, my mind was focused on the whole panorama of my past. There was no-one to tell, no-one in whom I could find some comfort." After fleeing to Mexico, she did have a chance to speak to delegations and reporters, but such encounters are often extremely formulaic, driven by pressure to raise awareness to what was taking place in Guatemala. Her time in Paris therefore was the first sustained opportunity Menchú had to process memories and survivor guilt. And what pours forth like a flood is a rich portrait of a complex, unique individual.

The final product—what became, first, *Me llamo Rigoberta Menchú y así me nació la conciencia* and then, in English translation, *I, Rigoberta Menchú*—is a composite of many people's work abridging, resequencing, and editing the raw material of Menchú's nearly week-long testimony. It is worth, then, reproducing here an extended portion of her interview, drawn from the session Menchú did with Arturo Taracena where she discusses one of the most disputed episodes of the book, the murder of her brother, Petrocinio. The selection is unabridged, translated as literally as possible to match Menchú's syntax and phrasing:

> His only sin was because since he was little he had participated with the community. He was kidnapped. My little brother was held captive for more than sixteen days by the enemy, who gave him great tortures, where they cut out his nails, they cut his tongue, they cut the bottom of his feet, they passed fire over all his body. The first wounds became infected, they swelled, they bled. Later they took out a, um, an announcement where they said there would be a punishment for the guerrillas. And we said, well, my mother said, "surely, my son is going to be there, surely he is going to be there." And we had to walk all the night and part of the day to go and see the place where there would be punishment for the guerrillas. And there my brother appeared. Together with twenty more tortured men. One woman where they had cut off her breast. And they had shaved her, they cut her, and nearly all the twenty men had different kinds of tortures. When we saw my brother it was difficult to recognize him, we doubted it was him because now he didn't seem like a human being. He seemed . . . We saw with our own eyes all this great suffering that they gave to our compañeros. We learned that among those that they called guerrillas was one of my brothers, they were neighbors, they were *catequistas* that we knew from elsewhere. And for us, we saw the savagery of these men, these humans who didn't realize, didn't have a heart to see all of the great pain of the people.

After a speech of more than three hours by the captain, and with every pause that he made in his speech they would beat the tortured ones, order the troops to hit them, forced them to stand up by beating them with sticks, and they couldn't stand up because of all their pain, they immediately fell to the floor. They bled. A uniformed soldier dressed in green came, when the captain had finished his speech, and cut the cloths off the tortured because now they couldn't take them [the clothes] off because they were stuck on top of the wounded. And they cut off their cloths, they took them, and when we saw the all the bodies they were disfigured. They didn't have the form of a human body. That is when they dragged them, closer, and piled them together in the place. They threw gasoline on them and burned them. We saw there that my own little brother was not dead. Many still shouted and many, though they cut off their breathing, didn't die. The bodies jumped. Unfortunately in our lands, in our places, there is no potable water. There was no public fountain to quickly get water to put out the fire that burned over the bodies of the dead. The neighbors had to run to get water. They went to look for water, and the fire was almost out when they returned. The army brazenly said Long Live the Army! Long Live Power! Long Live Lucas! Death to the Guerrillas! Those were their slogans. But we knew it was a humble people shouting for their just cause. My father was there, my mother was there, we were all there and my mother still embraced the body of my burned little brother. But not only was it us, but all the people was there crying, and, um, nobody else, we couldn't say anything else. And all the people had a hatred for the army, but that hatred we couldn't demonstrate by killing them as they kill us. But that was a hatred we were going to take with us to the struggle, a struggle for all and not against any group. There we watched, there we mourned the body of the dead. The following day they were buried, and whole town cried and went to bury the bodies. Later we returned to our

house and we seemed drunk because we couldn't believe what
we had seen. It seemed like a dream. Or it seemed, it seemed
like a *telenovela*.[11]

---

11. From the Elisabeth Burgos-Debray Papers, Box 1, Hoover
Archives. The original Spanish:

Su único delito era porque desde pequeño estaba participando
con la comunidad. Fue secuestrado. Estuvo mi hermanito más
de 16 días bajo poder del enemigo donde le dieron grandes
torturas, donde le cortaron las uñas, le cortaron la lengua, le
cortaron la planta de los pies, y le pasaron fuego encima de
todo su cuerpo. Los primeros heridos estaban infectados, estaban hinchados, echaba sangre. Luego sacan un, er, un anuncio
donde decían que iba a haber un castigo para los guerrilleros.
Y nosotros dijimos pues, "de seguro él iba a estar mi hijo,"
decía mi madre, "de seguro el iba a estar." Y tuvimos que cami-
nar toda la noche, parte del día para ir a ver el lugar donde
iba a haber castigo para los guerrilleros. Y ahí apareció mi
hermanito. Junto con 20 hombres más torturados. Una mujer
donde le habían quitado el pecho. Y le habían rasurado, le
habían cortado, y casi los 20 hombres tenían diferentes clases
de torturas. Cuando vimos a mi hermanito, es difícil que lo
reconocimos, dudábamos si era el porque ya no se veía como
persona humano. Se veía . . . Vimos con nuestros propios ojos
todo ese gran sufrimiento que dieron a nuestros compañeros.
Adivinamos que los que ellos los que llamaban guerrilleros
era uno mis hermanos, eran vecinos, eran catequistas que nos
conocíamos en otros lugares. Y esta para nosotros, descar-
adamente vimos lo que es el salvajismo de esos hombres, esos
humanos, que ya no se dan cuenta, no tienen corazón para ver
todo ese gran dolor del pueblo.
    Después del discurso del capitán por más de tres horas, y
cada pausa que hacía en su discurso pegaban a los torturados, obligaban la tropa que los pegaban, que los paraban a

Before and after this passage, Menchú at times uses the singular, "*yo*," or "I." But here, relating her brother's murder, she refers to herself exclusively, and repeatedly, with plural verbs and the pronoun "*nosotros*," or "we," an illustration of what the historians Lutz and Lovell say is the resonance between Menchú's oral

---

puras palotazos, y ellos no se pararon por todos los dolores, inmediatamente se caían en el suelo. Echaban sangre. Iba un uniformado con uniforme [verde oliva?] luego cuando ya acaba el discurso del capitán, corta la ropa de los torturados ya que ya no podían sacarlos porque estaba pegado encima de los heridos. Y cortaron la ropa, los quitaron, y cuando vimos los cuerpos de todos eran desfigurados. No tenía ya forma de cuerpo humano. Y así es cuando los llevan arrastrado, acercaron, los amontonaron en el lugar. Y los echaron gasolina y los quemaron. Vimos ahí que hasta mi propio hermanito no se moría. Muchos todavía gritaron y muchos se les tapó la respiración pero no se morían. Brincaban los cadáveres. Y desgraciadamente en nuestras tierras, en nuestros lugares, no hay agua potable. No hay pila para buscar agua inmediatamente para apagar el fuego que se rociaba encima de los muertos de los cadáveres. De los vecinos tuvieron que ir corriendo a buscar agua. De que fueron a buscar el agua, ya casi estaba apagado el fuego cuando llegaron. El ejército sale con mucho lujo donde decía "¡Viva el ejército!", "¡Viva el poder!", "¡Viva Lucas!", "¡Que se mueran los guerrilleros!", esos eran sus consignas. Y sin embargo nosotros sabíamos que era un pueblo humilde que estaba gritando por su causa justa. Así es que estaba ahí mi padre, estaba mi madre, estábamos todos, y mi madre todavía abraza el cadáver de mi hermanito quemado. Pero no solo éramos nosotros, todo el pueblo estaba ahí llorando, y nadie mas, er, no podíamos decir otra cosa. Y todo el pueblo teníamos un odio hacia el ejército, pero aquel odio que no podemos demostrar matándoles igual como a nosotros nos matan, sino que era odio que nos iba a llevar

testimony and historic Mayan accounts of atrocities associated with the Spanish conquest (in contrast, both the Spanish- and English-language editions of the book record Menchú as using a mix of singular and plural tenses to describe Petrocinio's execution). The collective voice is perhaps Menchú's acknowledgement that she did not witness her brother's death but was repeating her family's account of what happened. She was synthesizing accounts of other, similar executions; or she was repeating what her family had told her about how her brother had died. Whatever the case, Menchú's first return to the singular tense following the above passage is not to reference herself but to quote her mother explaining why she is leaving home to commit herself to political work: "she said, 'I as a woman have the obligation to see, or to make public this living testimony that I have so that mothers don't suffer what I have suffered seeing a tortured son.' "

Also striking is how this passage contradicts the published version of Petrocinio's death in one key detail. In the Spanish and English editions, Menchú is recorded as saying that the soldiers shouted slogans only to cover their own cowardice as they withdrew in the face of the crowd's anger. The "people raised their weapons and rushed at the army," the book relates. But in the above interview, Menchú says the exact opposite, emphasizing the brazenness of the soldiers and the powerlessness of onlookers who "couldn't say anything," or do anything save cry, imagine vengeance, bury the bodies, and stagger home dazed. Perhaps at another moment during

---

hacia una lucha, una lucha por todo y no son en contra de un grupo. Ahí se vigilaba, ahí se veló el cadáver de los muertos. Al siguiente día fueron enterrados donde masivamente el pueblo lloraba y fue a enterrar los cadáveres. Luego regresamos en casa donde parecíamos borrachos porque no creíamos lo que vimos. Pareciera ser un sueño. O pareciero, o pareciera ser una telenovela.

that week of interviews Menchú narrated this event along the lines of the published version, where, as transcribed and edited, Petrocinio's death galvanizes the family into decisive action and resolve: "when we got home Father said: 'I'm going back to work.'" But here speaking with Taracena, Menchú's unabridged words convey little but desolation and helplessness—disassociation, or detachment not political commitment, as if it were a dream, or a soap opera.[12]

Though Menchú exalts Mayan life for political reasons, as well as out of genuine affection, a perceptive reader of her testimony will find a surface not so still, a struggle not only on behalf of family and community but against them. She sanctifies her father as a paragon of revolutionary virtue, for instance, yet she also reveals an emotionally conflictive relationship to a man she alternately renders as loving, determined, and nurturing but also quick to anger, prone to drink and despair, and

---

12. In the book, the chapters on the killings of her brother, father and mother are followed by lengthy, considered discussions of cultural practices and beliefs, feminism, political organizing, and the heroism of clandestine life. In this interview session, however, little of note comes after the murders. Within less than a minute of concluding her account of her brother's death, Menchú describes her father's murder in but two sentences: "Días después, cae mi padre en la embajada de España. Es también que lo queman vivo." Then comes the familiar account of her mother's torments: "Mi madre fue comido por perros, por zopilotes y otros animals que contribuyenron. Y así es lo cuidan más por cuatro meses para que se garantice que no se recoge parte de su cadáver." Menchú ends with a passing reference to the racism she experienced as a servant and some programmatic statements about struggle and justice, but noticeably absent is the kind of revolutionary protaganism highlighted by the book's arrangement.

ineffectual. And as her story unfolds and Menchú's world expands, from Chimel to Guatemala as a whole and then to Mexico and beyond, it becomes clear that her progress—in terms of what she discusses (her political education) and what she omits (her formal education, such as it was)—is largely made possible by the turmoil and dislocation she is denouncing. The dissonance that results is irrepressible. "Papa used to be . . . well, I don't mean foolish exactly because it's the thieves who steal our land who are foolish . . . Well, they asked my father to sign a paper but he didn't know what it said because he'd never learned to read or write," she recalls, in a passage where the transcribers apparently left the ellipses in to capture a hesitant criticism and an implied superiority.[13] It is a hint that Menchú wrestled not just with routine ambivalences of those who enjoy advantages not available to parents, but the singular fact that those advantages were part and parcel of the terror that took your parents lives and shattered your hometown.

In the midst of social decay, Menchú as a person comes into sharper focus. "I was in love many times," she says, and considering the inassimilable loss of her family she can be forgiven if her initial explanation for why she rejected marriage and children seems like pamphleteering. But it is soon revealed that

---

13. John Beverly, *Testimonio: On the Politics of Truth* (Minneapolis, 2004), 65, suggests *I, Rigoberta Menchú* be read as a "oedipal bildungsroman built around the working through of an Electra complex." For another discussion of *testimonio* as a literary and political form, and the politics surrounding this particular testimony, see Mary Louise Pratt, "*I, Rigoberta Menchú* and the 'Culture Wars' ", in *The Rigoberta Menchú Controversy,* Arturo Arias, ed., University of Minnesota Press, 2001. For the way Stoll's allegations played out in Guatemala, see Diane M. *Nelson, Reckoning: The Ends of War in Guatemala* (Durham, NC, 2009).

her position is less a choice than an effort to get some control over a situation that leaves her little choice. "It puts me into a panic," she admits, "I don't want to be a widow, or a tortured mother." By the end of her story, it is her mother—her body having been left to the vultures until "not a bit . . . was left, not even her bones"—who emerged as the defining parent. Menchú credited her with pointing to a strategy of emancipation not through collective action or cultural identity but an insurgency of the self, a rebellion against filial expectations. "I don't want to make you stop feeling a woman," Menchú recalls her saying, "but your participation in the struggle must be equal to that of your brothers. But you mustn't join just as another number . . . A child is only given food when he demands it. A child who makes no noise gets nothing to eat."

The revolution was defeated. But many of the human rights, indigenous, and peasant organizations that continue today to fight to democratize Guatemalan society were founded as popular-front organizations covertly linked to one or another rebel group. One of the lasting contributions of the insurgent organizations, particularly the Ejército Guerrillero de los Pobres and the Organización Revolucionaria del Pueblo en Armas, was to provide a school for critical thinking for poor Guatemalans, many of whom continue to be politically active. As theories of how to understand and act in the world, Marxism and liberation theology gave inhabitants of one of the most subjugated regions in the Americas a way to link their local aspirations to larger national and international movements and to make sense of the kind of everyday, routine forms of violence, as well as stunning displays of terror, that are documented in Menchú's book. It also gave them a means to insist on their consequence as human beings. What makes Menchú's testimony so extraordinary is how far her engagement with ideas clearly outstripped whatever orientation she might have received from organizers.

What she learned from her travails, she learned by her own impressive will and intelligence. Her interpretation of events broadly reflects the concerns of liberation theology, and at times it can sound mechanical. But it is clearly rooted in her personal grappling with the dilemmas of history and her own particular experience of power and powerlessness. "The world I live in is so evil, so bloodthirsty, that it can take my life away from one moment to the next," Menchú says, "so the only road open to me is our struggle, the just war. The bible taught me that."

If *I, Rigoberta Menchú* only served as a testament of a failed revolution, a moment in history when the highest collective ideals of liberation theology crashed headlong into the most vicious distillate of Cold War anti-communism, it would be a good book, still worth reading. But what made liberation theology, along with Latin America's New Left more broadly, so potent a threat in a place as inhumane as Guatemala in the 1970s was not just its concern with social justice but its insistence on individual human dignity. This combination of solidarity and insurgent individuality is the heart of Menchú's memoir, and that's what makes it a great, perhaps even immortal, book.

Greg Grandin
New York City
July 2009

CHAPTER ONE

Clarifying History: On the Guatemalan Truth Commission

Truth commissions are curious, contradictory bodies.[1] They often raise hope of justice symbolized by the Nuremberg Trials yet operate within the impoverished political possibilities that exist throughout much of the post–Cold War world. They are rarely accompanied by prosecutions and often do not have the authority to subpoena or sanction. Rather than serving as instruments of justice, their value is seen, in the words of the South African Truth and Reconciliation Commission, in their ability to construct a "historic bridge" between "a deeply divided past of untold suffering" and a "future founded on the recognition of human rights."[2] Over the last two decades, truth commissions have been established in, among other places, Ghana, Nigeria, Chad, East Germany, and East Timor, where, it is commonly asserted, they marked the border between what those societies were—intolerant, fevered, arbitrary—and what they hope they have become—peaceful, impartial, protective.

---

1. For a summation of the history and work of truth commissions, see Priscilla B. Hayner, *Unspeakable Truths: Confronting State Terror and Atrocity* (New York, 2000). For legal and ethical debates surrounding their work, see Robert I. Rotberg and Dennis Thompson, *Truth v. Justice: The Morality of Truth Commissions* (Princeton, NJ, 2000).

2. South Africa. Truth and Reconciliation Commission, *Truth and Reconciliation Commission of South Africa Report* (Cape Town, 1998), 1, chap. 5, par. 1.

Yet before being adopted as a universal rite to solem-
nize the distinction between political liberalism and diverse
forms of violent, unrepresentative regimes, official inquiries, what came to be generally known as "truth commissions," into human rights abuses indexed a unique moment
in Latin American history, as the decline of socialist movements crossed paths with ascendant efforts to consolidate
liberal constitutional rule. Often portrayed as a "transition to
democracy," Latin America's move away from military dictatorships in the 1980s was less a transition than it was a conversion to a particular definition of democracy. In the decades
after World War II, there prevailed throughout the continent
a social understanding of the term, described by Leslie Bethell
and Ian Roxborough as entailing a "commitment to popular,
more particularly working-class participation in politics, and
social and economic improvements for the poorer sections
of the population."[3] By the 1960s, the violent suppression of
the mass movements that stood behind this definition gave
way to, on the one hand, militant, often armed, efforts, such
as the Cuban Revolution, to restructure economic and social
relations and, on the other, repressive anti-communist dictatorships that came to rule much of the continent. Beginning
in the early 1980s and continuing over the next decade and
a half, one country after another emerged from this cycle of
crisis politics not only through a return to constitutionalism but also by abandoning social-democratic principles of
development and welfare, opening up their economies to the
world market, and narrowing their conception of democracy

---

3. Leslie Bethell and Ian Roxborough, eds., "Conclusion: The
Postwar Conjuncture in Latin America and its Consequences,"
*Latin America between the Second World War and the Cold War,
1944–1948* (Cambridge, 1992), 327–28.

to focus more precisely on political and legal rights rather than on social ones.[4]

First instituted in Bolivia in 1982 with the modest Comisión Nacional de Desaparecidos and in Argentina in 1983 with the more extensive Comisión Nacional sobre la Desaparición de Personas, state-sanctioned investigations into past episodes of political terror were one part of this transition's agenda to cultivate a notion of liberal citizenship that viewed the state not as a potential executor of social justice but as an arbiter of legal disputes and protector of individual rights. In their initial formulations in Bolivia and Argentina, truth commissions were to be supplemented with prosecutions of at least the worst atrocities. Yet in most countries, the military and its allies emerged victorious from the counterinsurgent wars of the 1970s and 1980s, disinclined to give up their self-assigned immunity. This intransigence brought about a shift in the logic that justified truth commissions, which moved their work out of the legal arena into the realms of ethics and emotions. Efforts to get at the "truth" of past episodes of political violence would have two functions, as José Zalaquett, a Chilean law professor who would go on to play an important role in Chile's Comisión Nacional de Verdad y Reconciliación, argued in 1988. They would, first, repair the psychic damage caused by repression and, second, prevent such repression from occurring in the future. These two goals were said to be mutually dependent, in that officially sanctioned inquiries into the past, followed by public acceptance of the conclusions of those inquiries, would not only heal wounds but also help lay the foundation of liberal tolerance and thus prevent

---

4. For the radicalization of post-war social democracy and its consequences, see Greg Grandin, *The Last Colonial Massacre: Latin America in the Cold War* (Chicago, 2004).

future transgressions. "The truth in itself is both reparation and prevention," Zalaquett believed.[5]

Truth commissions therefore, while technically charged with examining the specifics of individual acts of violence according to accepted norms of national and international jurisprudence, came in fact to be concerned with the larger historical meaning of collective political repression.[6] Their final reports distill a violent past into a manageable, lucid story, one that portrays terror as an inversion of a democratic society, a nightmarish alternative of what lies ahead if it does not abide by constitutional rules. Yet the jurists who designed Latin America's first truth commissions approached historical interpretation with ambivalence, overtly denying, covertly embracing its import. As political liberals, they were suspicious of any effort to impose, softly or severely, a universal conception of the common good or to use history to

---

5. In Lawrence Weschler, *A Miracle, A Universe: Settling Accounts with Torturers* (New York, 1990), 243–45.

6. Although methods and mandates differ from commission to commission, in general, commissions of inquiry into political violence in Latin America and elsewhere have gathered testimony from victims and witnesses in order to document the patterns by which state or non-state agents violated human rights recognized by either national or international law. Commissions then made individual decisions on each case, similar to a panel of voting judges. When the investigative period ended, the commissions issued final reports that quantified violations, generally with the aid of a statistical database, and assigned global institutional responsibility. For a discussion of procedural questions related to the work of truth commissions, see Sanford Levinson, "Trials, Commissions, and Investigating Committees: The Elusive Search for Norms of Due Process," in Rotberg and Thompson, eds., *Truth v. Justice.*

justify militancy. Their liberalism demanded an acceptance
of plural interpretations of the past.[7] But they also argued
that a dramatic affirmation of liberal values was needed in
order to prevent recurrences of state violence or institutional breakdown and they often turned to the past in order
to define these values. Truth commissions therefore had to
deal with history, but, being largely run by lawyers, they were
concerned that too close an attention to realms of human
activity comfortably associated with historical inquiry—an
examination, say, of economic interests and collective movements, or the unequal distribution of power in society—
might grant moral pardons or inflame political passions.[8]
In most truth commissions, history was not presented as a
network of causal social and cultural relations but rather as
a dark backdrop on which to contrast the light of tolerance
and self-restraint.

In other words, truth commissions, by presenting an interpretation of history as parable rather than as politics, largely
denied the conditions that brought them into being. In Latin
America, this meant portraying terror not as an extension
of a reactive campaign against social-democratic nationalist projects, nor as an essential element in the consolidation of a new neoliberal order, but as a breakdown of social
relations, as but one more instance in a repetitive cycle of
"interruptions in democratic rule" that had taken place

---

7. See the discussion in Mark J. Osiel, "Ever Again: Legal
Remembrance of Administrative Massacre," *University of
Pennsylvania Law Review* 144 (December 1995): 463–704, 501–520.

8. For example, of the forty-five individuals, not including secretaries and computer specialists, that staffed the Chilean
National Commission on Truth and Reconciliation, thirty-nine
were lawyers, law school graduates, or law students.

since independence in the early nineteenth century.[9] As such, truth commissions serve as modern-day instruments in the creation of nationalism and embody what Benedict Anderson describes as nationalism's enabling paradox: the need to forget acts of violence central to state formation that can never be forgotten. Among such acts, Anderson lists the Saint Bartholomew's Day and Paris Commune massacres in France, and, in the United States, the Civil War and the annihilation of Native Americans. To this inventory could be added the hundreds of thousands of individuals murdered, "disappeared," or tortured during Latin America's "dirty wars" of the 1970s and 1980s, victims of campaigns that put to a provisional end political conflicts and ideological debates over how society should be organized, particularly those concerning the relationship of the citizen to the state.[10] While such violence is an essential component of state consolidation, in order to serve the purpose of nationalism, it needs to be ritualized, as Anderson puts it, "remembered/forgotten as 'our own.'"[11] The jurists who designed Latin America's transition to democracy drew ethical instruction from violence in toto, but they refused, despite the protests of victims and their families, to sanction the collective political projects that were defeated by the violence.

This essay examines the role truth commissions play in "remembering/forgetting" exemplary terror, focusing on three examples, Argentina, Chile, and Guatemala. The

---

9. Carlos Nino, *Radical Evil on Trial* (New Haven, CT, 1996), 32.

10. For a definition of the Latin American Cold War as a struggle to define the relationship of the individual to society, see Grandin, *The Last Colonial Massacre*, 191–98.

11. Benedict Anderson, *Imagined Communities: Reflections on the Origins and Spread of Nationalism* (London, 1991), 206.

evolution in the way that each approached the past emerged from, and thus revealed, the limits of the assumptions that underwrote Latin America's turn toward constitutional rule and free-market policies, particularly assumptions regarding the relationship of violence to nationalism, state formation, and democratic rule. In the first instance, the intellectuals who designed Argentina's post-dictatorship human rights policy, while understanding political violence to be rooted in psychological and cultural patterns deeply entrenched in national history, refrained from making any historical judgment in either the trials or in the final report of the Comisión Nacional sobre la Desaparición de Personas (CONADEP). Criminal proceedings, it was believed, would serve as an alternative to dealing directly with the past, as their transparency and impartiality would contrast with the darkness and arbitrariness of the dictatorship years. In Chile, the second case, where the power of the military foreclosed the possibility of prosecutions, the Comisión Nacional de Verdad y Reconciliación had to confront history more explicitly. Yet the burden of reconciliation, which was now understood as the commission's primary mandate as reflected in its title, demands a conception of history that takes national cohesion as its starting premise and posits violence as resulting from the dissolution of that unity. The commission's final report, therefore, narrated the conflict leading to the 1973 coup that ended Chilean democracy and initiated Augusto Pinochet's seventeen-year reign as resulting from an unraveling of the institutional and normative protections that bind society together. While the institutional repression that followed the coup was subject to scrutiny, the coup itself was redeemed as a tragic but necessary intervention that prevented complete national collapse. Finally, in Guatemala, the Comisión para el Esclarecimiento Histórico (CEH), which released its final report in 1999, operated in an even more constricted political terrain than its predecessors. Deep social divisions destroyed the conceit that either the past could be healed or future abuses prevented by appeals to national reconciliation. The commission likewise found the procedures used by previous truth commissions insufficient to account for the intensity of the violence that took place during a more than three-decade-long civil war, which included an acute two-year phase of violence against Mayans that the commission ruled to be genocidal. The commission turned more fully to causal history to break out of this impasse. While it did posit authoritarianism, expressed in a virulent strain of racism, as propelling the violence, it situated this variable within a larger political economic framework and examined its radicalization in light of the imperatives of civil war. In so doing, it produced an analysis that understood terror not as a result of state decomposition, a failure of the institutions and morals that guarantee rights and afford protection, but rather as a component of state formation, as the foundation of the military's plan of national stabilization through a return to constitutional rule.[12]

*

12. The CEH's historical analysis has implications for postmodern debates surrounding the validity of narrative as such, a debate this essay will not directly touch on but which was explicitly addressed by the South African Truth and Reconciliation Commission. See Deborah Posel, "The TRC Report: What Kind of History? What Kind of Truth?" in *Commissioning the Past: Understanding South Africa's Truth and Reconciliation Commission*, Deborah Posel and Graeme Simpson, eds. (Johannesburg, 2001).

Following its defeat by England in the Malvinas War of 1982, the disgraced Argentine military gave up power after six years of rule based on political terror.[13] Even before his 1983 election, Raúl Alfonsín, of the center-left Unión Cívica Radical, convened a human rights kitchen cabinet of intellectuals, drawn mostly from the law school and philosophy department of the University of Buenos Aires, to plan the policy he would follow to address the violence of the past regime.[14] After taking office, Alfonsín and his advisors, the most influential of whom were law professors Carlos Nino and Jaime Malamud-Goti, designed a legal strategy that attempted to reconcile a number of concerns: the need to respond to the demands, backed by large, vociferous street demonstrations, for justice; the desire not to provoke the still-powerful military high command; and their own understanding of the function of criminal jurisprudence in a liberal society.[15] In the first formulations of human

---

13. Alejandro Dabat and Luis Lorenzano, *Argentina: The Malvinas and the End of Military Rule*, Ralph Johnstone, trans. (London, 1984).

14. A group of moral and legal philosophers from the United States, including Ronald Dworkin, Thomas Nagel, and Owen Fiss, also became involved in the transition process, as observers and advisors. Nino, *Radical Evil*, 84.

15. Mark Osiel, "The Making of Human Rights Policy in Argentina: The Impact of Ideas and Interests on a Legal Conflict," *Journal of Latin American Studies* 18 (May 1986): 135–80, 142. Both Carlos Nino and Jaime Malamud-Goti are the authors of a number of influential legal essays and books. See, for Nino, in addition to *Radical Evil*, *Los límites de la responsabilidad penal: Una teoría liberal del delito* (Buenos Aires, 1981), and *Ética y Derechos Humanos* (Buenos Aires, 1984). For Malamud-Goti: "Punishment and a Rights-Based Democracy," *Criminal Justice Ethics* 10, no. 2 (Summer/Fall 1991): 3–13, and *Game without End: State Terror and the Politics of Justice* (Norman, OK, 1996).

rights policy by these politician-scholars, the establishment of a truth commission was part of a larger strategy that was to include prosecutions. They did not believe, as many later came to accept, that the quest for punishment had to be weighed against the search for truth. Although the new government insisted on the need to limit the scope of prosecutions, trials were nonetheless essential to their primary goal of preventing a return to military and repressive rule.[16] In setting their human rights agenda, Alfonsín and his advisors drew heavily from ethical social theory influenced by Emile Durkheim. Legal procedures, in their view, were more than agreed-upon rules to settle unavoidable conflicts. Rather, they formalized a common social cohesion, a cohesion that would strengthen and be strengthened by the application of liberal democratic

---

16. According to Nino, Alfonsín's primary objective was the "reinstatement of the rule of law and the prevention of such human rights violations in the future. Impunity was incompatible with these principles. While the pursuit of truth would be unrestricted, the punishment would be limited, based on deterrent rather than retributive considerations." Nino, *Radical Evil*, 68. By "retributive," Nino is referring to an opinion that "the evil caused by the violations of human rights should be met by the closest possible equivalent." It is a term that Alfonsín and his legal advisors generally used to describe what they felt was the absolutist position of human right groups that, "invok[ing] Kant," asked "for the punishment of every last individual responsible for the atrocities, even if society were at the brink of dissolution." *Radical Evil*, 136. Prior to their becoming advisors to Alfonsín, Nino and Eduardo Rabossi, a member of the CONADEP, both adhered to retributive views similar to human rights organizations; see Nino, *Los límites de la responsabilidad penal*, and Rabossi, *La justificación moral del castigo* (Buenos Aires, 1976).

procedures.[17] Nino argued that the prosecution of military officials was required "in order to inculcate in the collective conscience and in the consciences of the groups concerned that no sector of the population stands above the law."[18] Trials would contrast the openness and fairness of liberalism with the secrecy and impunity of authoritarianism, thus building support for democracy. The establishment of a commission of inquiry was to be an important first step in the eliciting of public support for criminal prosecutions: it would establish the scope and institutional responsibility for atrocities, prepare preliminary cases for indictment, and help families of victims learn the fate of their disappeared relatives.

Alfonsín announced the formation of the Comisión Nacional sobre la Desaparición de Personas (CONADEP) within days of his inauguration. While indictments and trials were to be limited to those who either ordered the repression or conducted it with excessive cruelty, exempting lower level officers and soldiers who strictly obeyed orders, CONADEP was to provide a full as possible account of "disappearances," the military's preferred method of disposing of perceived enemies. Between December 1983 and September 1984, the commission collected thousands of testimonies and visited hundreds of detention and torture centers and clandestine graves. CONADEP presented its final report in November, documenting the disappearance of 8,960 Argentines, but predicted that that number would rise with further investi-

---

17. Carlos Nino, "Transition to Democracy, Corporatism and Constitutional Reform in Latin America," *University of Miami Law Review* 44 (1989–1990): 129–64, 136.

18. Osiel, "Ever Again," 478–89, describes Durkheim's influence on the Argentine jurists.

gation.[19] At the end of its work, the commission handed 1,086 cases to the judiciary and recommended that the government create a permanent office to continue filing cases in the courts.

While *Nunca Más* (Never Again), as the published version of CONADEP's report was called, made no attempt to place political disappearances within an historical context, history was very much on the minds of the people who conceived the commission. In response to the spread, starting in the late 1960s, of military regimes throughout the continent, southern cone social scientists began to elaborate an analytical framework influenced by both Weberian sociology and Marxism to explain Latin America's seemingly chronic resort to military dictatorships. Scholars such as Argentina's Guillermo O'Donnell and Brazil's Fernando Henrique Cardoso focused on the political and economic variables that contributed to patterns of bureaucratization along strongly authoritarian, militaristic lines.[20] Transitional-justice intellectuals borrowed from this framework yet departed from its institutional and economic focus to stress instead psychological disruptions supposedly caused by the modernization of social relations. Malamud-Goti, for example, argued that political violence erupted from a "dictatorial mind" chronic to Argentine history.[21] Nino, especially influenced by Durkheim and his concept of anomie to describe how the corrosion of social institutions

---

19. Argentina. Comisión Nacional Sobre la Desaparición de Personas, *Nunca más: Informe de la Comisión Nacional Sobre la Desaparición de Personas* (Buenos Aires, 1984).

20. See Guillermo O'Donnell, *Modernization and Bureaucratic-Authoritarianism* (Berkeley, CA, 1973), and Fernando Henrique Cardoso, *Autoritarismo e democratizaçë* (Rio de Janeiro, 1975).

21. Malamud-Goti, *Game without End*, 183.

by the forces of modernization led to a psychological tolerance of authoritarianism, identified a number of psychic or
ideational factors to explain Argentina's descent into terror:
"ideological dualism" led to a clash between secular, universal liberalism and "closed, organic" conservatism; a tendency
toward "corporatism" invested the Catholic Church, the
armed forces, and business groups with an inordinate
amount of power; "anomie" contributed to a "disregard for
social norms, including the law."[22] In his public pronounce-
ments, Alfonsín invoked similarly tautological explanations
to account for the violence that took place during the previous regime.

The post-junta government designed a human rights
policy aimed at breaking these historically rooted "insidi-
ous cultural patterns."[23] Through trials and the commission, Alfonsín and his advisors hoped to summon images
of a past gone awry both to establish a common set of social
values and to provide a sober warning about what lay ahead
if Argentines did not abide by institutional procedures. Yet
they believed that to look to the past was dangerous, for
while law may be adversarial in process, history is divisive in
its conclusions.

---

22. Nino, *Radical Evil*, 44–46. For "anomie," see Emile
Durkheim, *Suicide* (New York, 1951), 250–54. In *Un país al margen
de la ley: Estudio de la anomia como componente del subdesarrollo
argentino* (Buenos Aires, 1992), Nino lays out in detail his understanding of the historical relationship between institutions,
values, authoritarianism, and violence, drawing directly from
Durkheim as well as from subsequent modernization theorists,
such as Samuel Huntington and Seymour Martin Lipset, and Latin
American sociologists such as O'Donnell and Cardoso.

23. Malamud-Goti, *Game without End*, 183.

"Great catastrophes are always instructive," wrote CONADEP's chairperson, the Argentine novelist Ernesto Sabato, who in a graceful prologue to the commission's final report largely steered clear of history to extract from the sadism of the military the lesson that "only democracy can save people from such a horror, only democracy can protect the sacred, basic rights of man." Argentina's jurists saw themselves as mediating between dangerously volatile social groups that had competing yet equally passionate investments in assigning historical meaning to the "dirty war." Grassroots human rights organizations, such as the Madres de Plaza de Mayo, founded in 1979 by relatives of the "disappeared" to protest state terror, along with members and sympathizers of the insurgent Montoneros, an urban guerrilla group operating in the 1970s made up of supporters of the late Juan Domingo Perón, insisted on interpreting the war as a struggle to achieve social justice in the context of a society that was deeply unjust. The military, for its part, demanded that human rights violations be understood as painful but necessary measures taken to defend the homeland against foreign subversion.[24] In response, the Alfonsín government adopted what eventually became known as the "doctrine of the two demons": a refusal to attach historical importance to the repression conducted by the previous regime apart from the belief that political violence is a symptom of illiberal intolerance. The political extremism of both the military and the armed Left was held equally responsible for Argentina's plunge into chaos. "During the 1970s," goes the first sentence of the report, "Argentina was torn by terror from both the extreme right and the far left"— this despite the fact that the violence catalogued by *Nunca Más*

---

24. Horacio Verbitsky, *La posguerra sucia: Un análisis de la transición* (Buenos Aires, 1985), 30.

was nearly exclusively committed by the military against, as Sabato's prologue admits, "trade unionists fighting for better wages, members of student unions, journalists who did not support the regime, psychologists and sociologists simply for belonging to suspicious professions, young pacifists, nuns and priests who had taken the teachings of Christ to poor neighborhoods, the friends of these people, too, and the friends of friends." Many have noted the influence of Max Weber's "Politics as Vocation" essay, with its advice that politics above all else entailed a "responsibility towards the future," on southern cone jurists.[25] In particular, Alfonsín's refusal to be drawn into historical debate echoes Weber's suggestion, made after World War I, that the best way to avoid future conflict was to avoid imposing a judgment on the causes of the war, which would then force contending parties to dissipate their passions arguing the war "ad absurdum."[26] Weber's rejection of attempts to justify political militancy through appeals to an "ethic of ultimate ends" reverberates in Nino's condemnation of the Argentine insurgency as "the product of an epistemic elitism regarding facts and morality." "Left-wing terrorism,"

---

25. For the influence of this essay on transitional-justice jurists, see José Zalaquett, "Introduction to the English Edition," in Chile. National Commission on Truth and Reconciliation, *Report of the Chilean National Commission on Truth and Reconciliation,* Phillip E. Berryman, trans., 2 vols. (Notre Dame, IN, 1993), 1: xxx. For Weber's influence on the South African Truth and Reconciliation Commission, see Posel, "The TRC Report," 159; for his influence in Uruguay's return to constitutionalism, see Weschler, *A Miracle, A Universe,* 186.

26. Max Weber, "Politics as Vocation," in *From Max Weber: Essays in Sociology,* H. H. Gerth and C. Wright Mills, eds. and trans. (New York, 1946), 120.

Nino writes, provoked "foreseeable consequences" that were "far worse than the evils it sought to eradicate."[27]

Such a position expectedly angered those who suffered or committed acts of violence in the name of a higher ideal, either in pursuit of social justice or in defense of the nation. Julie Taylor has suggested that the legalistic procedures of CONADEP, which abstracted human rights violations from the dynamics of social power and conflict, reproduced the logic of a repression that was intended to break down networks of political solidarity. She writes that all "who passed through this process, then, accused and accusers—actors in highly political dramas where they had represented clashing world views and collective strategies for implementing them— were refigured as innocent or transgressing individuals with individual rights and obligations." The truth commission's "opposition of the order of law and the chaos of violence further led to the omission of collective motivation not only of victimizers . . . but of victims as well, who were defended as individuals whose human rights had been violated rather than as political activists."[28]

That was exactly the point. During the first years of Argentina's transition to democratic rule, the trials—which barred any reference to political ideals or collective identities from being introduced as testimony—were to serve as the primary theater of procedural conflict in the new liberal order. For Nino, prosecutions were needed to dilute the "corporatism" that he held responsible for Argentine authoritarianism,

---

27. Nino, *Radical Evil*, 170.
28. Julie Taylor, "Body Memories: Aide-Memoires and Collective Amnesia in the Wake of the Argentine Terror," in *Body Politics: Disease, Desire, and the Family*, Michael Ryan and Avery Gordon, eds. (Boulder, CO, 1994), 197.

to "enable victims of human rights abuses to recover their self-respect as holders of legal rights"—not as members of social groups engaged in cooperative struggle.[29] To the degree that history was needed to evoke a brutal past to contrast with a dispassionate future, this contrast would be represented by the impartiality and transparency of the court procedures. Trials, Malamud-Goti writes, were to "provide a particular way, a means, to come to terms with the past, to instill individual responsibility, to establish the scope and depth of the truth, and, most of all, to write the country's recent history in the language of moral responsibility."[30]

The new government underestimated both the desire for retributive justice and the obstinacy of the armed forces. Alfonsín took office in December 1983. Within a year, victims and victims' families had filed approximately 2,000 criminal complaints against the military.[31] In 1985, the "big trial," as the prosecution of a number of high military officials was called, resulted in the conviction of General Jorge Videla and Admiral Emilio Massera, who both received life sentences. But by 1986, as criminal investigations continued, Alfonsín came under increasing pressure from the military. In the face of a series of failed but formidable coup attempts, he passed the "full stop" law, which imposed an absolute cut-off date for the trials. In 1987, Alfonsín called a halt to military prosecutions and signed the law of "due obedience," which allowed military officers to argue in their defense that they "had acted

29. Nino, *Radical Evil*, 147.

30. Malamud-Goti, *Game without End*, 183.

31. Alejandro M. Garro and Henry Dahl, "Legal Accountability for Human Rights Violations in Argentina: One Step Forward and Two Steps Backward," *Human Rights Law Journal* 38 (1987): 283–344, 311n.115.

under orders and thus were not punishable."[32] Full capitulation came in 1990 when Carlos Menem, Alfonsín's successor, pardoned in the name of "national reconciliation" all those either awaiting trial or already convicted, including Videla and Massera.[33]

In that same year that Menem pardoned the junta leaders, Chilean dictator Augusto Pinochet left office. In March, Patricio Aylwin was elected to the presidency under more constrained conditions than was Alfonsín, and made no effort to prosecute military officers for human rights violations committed during Pinochet's seventeen-year dictatorship. Despite losing the plebiscite, which would have allowed him to continue in power, Pinochet, unlike the Argentine military, ended his tenure much on his own terms. An amnesty law protected those responsible for political repression, while Pinochet remained in charge of the military and a number of his associates became senators-for-life.

Aylwin convened the Comisión Nacional de Verdad y Reconciliación, known more commonly as the Rettig Commission from its president Raúl Rettig, in 1990 to investigate political disappearances and extrajudicial executions that occurred during Pinochet's rule. As in Argentina, the commission was to mark the transition from dictatorial to procedural rule and to help re-establish political pluralism and liberal morals—re-establish in the sense that prior to

---

32. Nino, *Radical Evil*, 101. See Kathryn Lee Crawford, "Due Obedience and the Rights of the Victims: Argentina's Transition to Democracy," *Human Rights Quarterly* 12, no. 1 (1990): 17–52.

33. Mark Osiel, *Mass Atrocity, Ordinary Evil, and Hannah Arendt: Criminal Consciousness in Argentina's Dirty War* (New Haven, 2001), 20.

Pinochet's September 11, 1973, coup that resulted in the death of Salvador Allende, Chile was one of Latin America's most stable democracies. José Zalaquett, a professor of ethics and human rights at the University of Chile and a prominent member of the commission, writes that the commission was to "help to create a consensus concerning events about which the community is deeply divided . . . The purpose of truth is to lay the groundwork for a shared understanding of the recent crisis and how to overcome it."[34] The Rettig Commission, however, unlike in Argentina, was not part of a larger policy of indictments and trials. Chile, in other words, retained the notion that official inquiries into past abuses were needed to reinforce social solidarity but jettisoned, due to political exigencies, the required mechanism that, according to Nino and others, bestowed those inquires with legitimacy: the ability to hold the worst abusers legally accountable.

The shift in emphasis from truth and justice to, in the words of President Aylwin, "truth, and justice as far as possible," brought history to the fore.[35] Absent the possibility of using legal procedures to undermine historically derived "invidious cultural patterns," recent Chilean history had to be confronted directly rather than through the proxy of trials. Zalaquett writes that "our report was basically about facts and their circumstances. Of course these are ethically relevant facts. They signify the transgression of fundamental societal values." The commission, he continues, "was

---

34. José Zalaquett, "Truth Commissions: A Comparative Assessment," Interdisciplinary Discussion, Harvard Law School (May 1996).

35. Militza García, "Patricio Aylwin: El Adversario Clave," *Qué Pasa* (Santiago, Chile), September 5, 2003.

the cornerstone of a transitional policy aimed at the moral (and political) reconstruction of our society after a period of tragic breakdown ... To that end we felt we had to refer not to human rights violations and acts of violence but also to the ideological/doctrinary basis which prescribed, directly lead to, or attempted to legitimate such deeds."[36] The Rettig Report explicitly laid out, through a description of events leading up to the 1973 coup, a vision of the past similar to Nino's and Malamud-Goti's intentionally vague conjectures concerning the roots of political violence.[37] In the case of Chile, a lawyerly ambivalence toward historical conjecture augmented the opacity of such an approach, as manifested in the final report's disclaimers that the commission was "aware that all events are subject to diverse and contradictory versions and interpretations" and that while it recognized that the "crisis has deep roots, of a socioeconomic character, it would go beyond its mandate to explore them."[38] Adding to this modesty was a concern that too close an attention to past conflicts could be used to excuse or justify political violence. The Rettig Report, Zalaquett states, is a "circumscribed historical approach. It is the history of doctrinary

---

36. Zalaquett, personal communication, February 2001.

37. The report does not cite any primary or secondary sources to indicate how its accounting of "some characteristics of the climate" that preceded the coup was compiled. It is commonly known that conservative Chilean historian and commission member Gonzalo Vial, who had previously served in Pinochet's government, wrote the first draft of the section describing events leading to the coup.

38. Chile. Comisión Nacional de Verdade y Reconciliación, *Informe de la Comisión Nacional de Verdad y Reconciliación*, 3 vols. (Santiago, 1991) 1: 33, 38.

justification of ethically unacceptable means in political action."[39]

The starting point of the commission's historical section is the "extreme polarization" engendered by the Cold War. In Latin America, the 1959 Cuban Revolution "overflowed its borders" and pitted throughout the continent "Cuban-Soviet 'insurgency' against North American 'counterinsurgency,'" with Chile being "no exception."[40] The 1970 election of socialist Salvador Allende, who presided over a coalition government of left parties that pursued an agenda of nationalization and land reform, initiated what the commission described as the "final phase" of this polarization in Chile. The Rettig Report compellingly describes a breakdown of state sovereignty during Allende's tenure, which contributed to the propulsion of ideas and actions toward an ever greater militancy. Centrist and rightist groups, fearing that Allende had betrayed the state's very reason for existence—the protection of private property—applied tactics to make the country "ungovernable." Left political parties, even those who rejected armed struggle and remained committed to electoral politics, became "seduced" by those who insisted on the "inevitability" of confrontation. Violence "was spurred on," the report writes, "because, as a result of deep polarization, each individual believed that they were transgressing the law only in response to, and as a defense against, someone else who had already done so . . . The only defense (they thought) was self-defense, thus spreading the idea of irregular armed groups in both city and countryside to defend the ownership of properties and companies and personal security."

---

39. Zalaquett, personal communication, February 2001.

40. The following quotations come from *Informe de la Comisión*, 1: 35, 36, 38.

Yet while the passions, particularly "fear" and "hatred," are
amply represented in this history of "ethically unacceptable
means in political action," absent is any discussion of interests and power. The final report captures well the contingent
exigencies of political crisis, yet its refusal to analyze the
"socioeconomic" roots of that crisis led it to present militancy in the passive tense, as latent in the body politic and
called forth by forces beyond Chile's borders: national political movements and parties became "ideologized" by global
polarization and began to insist on "total models for society"
unable to admit any but the "slightest modifications, post-
ponements, or negotiations"; individuals and groups lost faith
in democratic institutions and began to advocate violence and
force as a means to power; "extreme groups of whatever political persuasion do not need a reason or pretext for becoming
armed. And so the fever spread throughout Chile."

Chilean historians have criticized the report for its insistence on the need to establish moral equivalency between
the Left and the Right, and for ignoring Allende's demonstrated commitment to political pluralism and willingness
to compromise.[41] The report is evidently more sympathetic
to the fears that motivated opposition to Allende in defense
of private property than to those of the "extreme left political groups" that spread an "ideology of armed struggle." Yet
the commission went further. A depiction of Chile as caught
in the maelstrom of world politics and a reflexive rendition
of ideological hardening led to the suggestion that the military's overthrow of Allende prevented a larger catastrophe:
military officers, divided between constitutionalists and those
who opposed Allende, "had to consider the possibility that

41.   Sergio Grez Toso and Gabriel Salazar Vergara, eds.,
Manifiesto de historiadores (Santiago, 1999).

their failure to act might entail a greater evil: civil war, as a result of their own internal division." History here fulfilled its exculpatory potential, for the forces that drove the military to intervene were inexorable: "Until their decisive intervention in September 1973, the armed forces and the police, notwithstanding the ideologies and debates stirring in their ranks, stayed out of the crisis and maintained their professionalism, discipline, obedience to the civilian power and political neutrality, as assigned to them by the Constitution. Nevertheless, the very exacerbation of the crisis—slowly but surely, continually and increasingly—drew them away from this role."[42]

The historical sensibility that motivated the Rettig Commission approximates that of the Argentine jurists. In both, visions of the past were less historically specific than mythically timeless—touchstones of unacceptable worldviews and behavior by which to measure a democratic society. In the case of Chile, a refusal to examine ideological polarization as mediated by political interests and social power provides a no less psychologically determined account of a friend-enemy disassociation than that offered by Nino or Malamud-Goti.

---

42. *Informe de la Comisión*, 1: 39–40. The report was obliquely referencing a plan by a left-wing group not formally part of the Popular Unity coalition to organize support for Allende within the military to forestall a coup. See John Dinges, *The Condor Years: How Pinochet and His Allies Brought Terrorism to Three Continents* (New York, 2004), 43–44. The report also lists other reasons the coup could be interpreted as a defense of national sovereignty, including the escalating disruptions of public order, the threat such disruptions posed to the country's food supply, and the "whetting foreign appetites" eager to take advantage of political instability (a reference to territorial conflicts with Argentina and Peru).

"The dictatorial mind," writes Malamud-Goti, "sets itself up to generate this split: allies versus foes, conspiratorial accounts of political reality that turn themselves into a cause for further authoritarianism."[43] In the case of Chile, absent the possibility of pursuing retributive justice that could fortify the rule of law, the Rettig Report emphasized the contrast between the dispassionate procedural liberalism of a restored democracy and the ideological rigidity and intolerance not only of the Pinochet regime but also of the events claimed to have necessitated that regime. In the process, the coup is revalued as a required moment of primal violence that both rescued the nation from dissolution, a "tragic breakdown," as Zalaquett put it, and justified the constraints in which the new democracy operated.

Based on the collection of over 8,000 testimonies from victims and their relatives, Guatemala's Comisión para el Esclarecimiento Histórico (CEH) concluded, in 1999, that over the course of a nearly four-decade civil war that pitted the state against a Left insurgency, the military had committed 626 massacres and was responsible for 93 percent of human rights abuses, including roughly 200,000 political murders. The commission blamed the guerrillas for 3 percent of the violations and 32 massacres. Yet *Guatemala: Memoria del silencio*, as the CEH's final twelve-volume report is titled, goes well beyond divvying out responsibility for the violence to the state and the guerrillas. Starting with an introduction that displays little of the epistemological hesitation of similar bodies, the CEH provides statistical evidence of extreme social inequality—the country's health, education, literacy, and nutritional indicators are among the most unjust in the world despite an

43. Malamud-Goti, *Game without End*, 187.

abundance of national wealth—and spends the rest of its first volume chronicling the "causes and origins" of Guatemala's armed conflict.

Administered by the United Nations, the CEH was staffed mostly by lawyers drawn from the transnational human rights community, many of whom were from or had previous advocacy experience in southern cone countries. They shared with their Argentine and Chilean counterparts a reluctance to contextualize human rights violations either in reference to social inequalities or historical struggles. Yet a number of factors pushed them in that direction.[44] The most important was the success of the counterinsurgency. Unlike in Argentina and Chile, Guatemala's truth commission was not negotiated by civilian reformers hoping to broker a guided transition to democracy. In Guatemala, that "transition" took place a decade earlier, under the tight supervision of the military as the civil war continued. Rather, the one-page document that established the CEH was an afterthought, negotiated by an enervated guerrilla leadership and a triumphant army high command as part of peace talks that in 1996 finally drew the war to an official close. The commission did not have the power to subpoena witnesses or records, and its final report could not "individualize responsibility"—that is, name names—nor could it be used for prosecutions.[45]

---

44. Head commissioner Christian Tomuschat describes his interpretation of the CEH mandate in "Clarification Commission in Guatemala," *Human Rights Quarterly* 23, no. 2 (2001): 233–58.

45. The accord is in the commission's final report: Comisión para el Esclarecimiento Histórico, *Guatemala: Memoria del silencio*, 12 vols. (Guatemala City, 1999), 1: 23–26. (Hereafter, CEH, *Memoria del silenció*.)

In a strategic avoidance of potential deal-breaking specifics, negotiators left vague other aspects of the commission's work. Unlike the strict mandates of CONADEP and the Rettig Commission, the CEH's instructions did not define the crimes to be examined, the period to be considered, or the commission's methodology. This ambiguity, it turns out, allowed the commission to define its work broadly and to use social science and historical analysis to a greater extent than did previous truth commissions. The diversity and composition of the CEH's staff and three-member commissariat, comprised of both foreigners and nationals, likewise contributed to a more vital engagement with historical analysis. Confronted with ongoing social cleavages and an unrepentant military and oligarchy, foreigners, including head commissioner Christian Tomuschat, a German human rights jurist, and Marcie Mersky, who edited the final report, had little incentive to turn the CEH into an incurious promoter of nationalism. Guatemalan nationals, drawn from the country's embattled human rights movement and shut out of the negotiations that brought the CEH into being, had little faith that an affirmation of shared social values would be sufficient to overcome the injustices of the past. In addition, an emerging pan-Mayan cultural rights movement—in many ways the most vibrant element of Guatemala's post-war civil society—was beginning to interpret not just the war but all of national history through the prism of racism and demanding that the CEH do the same. The influence of this movement led to the appointment of Otilia Lux de Cotí, a Mayan educator, to the commission. Lux, along with Mayan rights groups, pushed for an investigation of genocidal intent to describe the military's targeting of indigenous communities between 1981 and 1983, an investigation that likewise contributed to the CEH's turn toward historical analysis.[46]

As did southern cone jurists, the CEH drew on theories that focus on the effects of skewed modernization to explain authoritarianism and political violence, tracing the roots of a "political culture where intolerance defined the totality of social interaction" back to the Spanish colonial period.[47] In Argentina and Chile, though, there was no attempt to think

---

46. From commencement of operations in August 1997 to the issuance of its final report in February 1999, the CEH drew on multiple resources to compile its historical section: individual testimonies; US declassified documents; secondary sources; "context reports" from fourteen regional field offices; inputs by a group of Guatemalan social scientists convened by the commission to serve in an advisory capacity; "illustrative cases" described in detail (as opposed to the 8,000 "ordinary cases," based on testimony and not investigated at great length). When the commission moved to the writing-up stage, four teams—corresponding to the four major sections of *Memoria del silencio* (1. an interpretation of the "causes and origins" of the armed conflict; 2. a description of the techniques of violence and the establishment of institutional responsibility; 3. an account of the social consequences of the violence; 4. the elaboration of a series of policy recommendations)—synthesized this voluminous information. A team of editors then produced the final report which, unlike the Rettig Report, is copiously cited. Reluctance on the part of the lawyers who ran the CEH to formulate preliminary working hypotheses, however, led to a certain degree of methodological incoherence and a figure-it-out-as-needed approach to data collection, as Marcie Mersky, the coordinator of the final report, describes in "Some Initial Thoughts on the Commission for Historical Clarification in Guatemala," a paper presented at Yale University (April 7, 1999).

47. CEH, *Memoria del silencio*, 1: 79.

through the connection between intolerance and terror. Psychological variables allegedly responsible for political violence, such as, say, anomie, are simply deduced without any specific attention to how radicalization emerges from the interplay between ideas, social structures, and political interests. The CEH, in contrast, presented intolerance as the product of polarization and not its a priori cause. The prohibition against naming names led to vague phrasing and contorted sentence constructions, yet *Memoria del silencio* nonetheless insisted on examining the mediation between what it identifies as systemic causes of state violence—economic exploitation, racism, and political exclusion—and the ideas and actions associated with challenges and defenses of that system.

Since the end of the nineteenth century, according to the CEH, "the landed class," particularly coffee planters, "imposed its economic interests on the state and society."[48] Planters gobbled up vast amounts of land and relied on the state to ensure the cheap supply of labor, mostly Mayan Indians from highland communities. A series of forced labor laws combined with land loss to "increase the economic subordination" of Mayans and poor ladinos (Guatemalans not considered Mayan). This model of coercive development intensified forms of colonial exploitation, racism, and authoritarianism and militarized the republican state, which devoted itself to enforcing labor servitude. The mainspring, according to the commission, of the Guatemalan crisis was the conflict between efforts to reform society and measures taken in its defense: "State violence has been fundamentally aimed against the excluded, the poor, and the Maya, as well as those who struggled in favor of a just and more equitable society . . .

---

48. Ibid., 1: 81.

Thus a vicious circle was created in which social injustice led to protest and subsequently to political instability, to which there were always only two responses: repression or military coups." Confronted with movements demanding "economic, political, social, or cultural change the state increasingly resorted to terror in order to maintain social control. Political violence was thus a direct expression of structural violence."[49]

This dynamic eased and even reversed for a ten-year period starting in 1944, when two reformist administrations attempted to democratize Guatemala's economy and polity by ending forced labor, legalizing unions, enacting workplace protections, establishing a social security and public health care system, expanding the vote, and passing a far-reaching land reform. The CEH's analysis of the Central Intelligence Agency's (CIA) 1954 coup that ended this democratic decade stands in opposition to the Rettig Commission, which blamed Allende's 1973 ouster on Cold War polarization. *Memoria del silencio,* while careful to document the US role in the coup, focused squarely on domestic political and class interests. Threatened by the rapid extension of rights to the country's disenfranchised, the "defenders of the established order," identified in the report as planters, the military, and the Catholic Church, joined with a middle class threatened by increased peasant and indigenous mobilization to oppose the government of Jacobo Arbenz, the reform period's second president.[50] And while the Rettig Report salvaged the military's assumption of power in Chile as a moment of nationalist sacrifice, the CEH presented the CIA's 1954 intervention as a national "trauma" that had a "collective political effect" on a generation of young, reform-minded Guatemalans. "So

49. Ibid., 5: 21–22.
50. Ibid., 1: 103–5.

drastic was the closing of channels of participation and so extensive was the recourse to violence" by those opposed to democracy, *Memoria del silencio* argued, that it is "considered one of causes of the guerrilla insurgency" that roiled Guatemala for nearly four decades. The overthrow of Arbenz reinitiated Guatemala's "exclusivist dynamic," and the state once again put "itself at the bidding of a minority at the expense of the majority."[51] Expectations raised and struggles fought during the ten years of democracy reverberated throughout Guatemala's subsequent civil war, and the CEH traced a number of the human rights violations that it recounts in detail back to the 1954 coup.

The sharpest break between *Memoria del silencio* and its predecessors was not the CEH's methodological description of unfolding crisis politics but its analysis of the relationship between terror and state formation. In most truth commissions, as well as in the commentaries that justify them, the morals that allow political terror to take hold are taken as the inverse of liberal pluralism. Tolerance is mirrored by intolerance, civic trust by anomie. Where there should be proceduralism and open-mindedness, there is arbitrariness and fanaticism. In many accounts of crisis, what makes possible the prevalence of these dark values is state and social decay, a weakening of the institutions that generate the norms that hold society together.

The CEH, in contrast, took a different approach in its understanding of Guatemala's descent into terror, particularly in its analysis of an intense two-year phase of violence. Of the 626 massacres committed by the military or its allies documented by the CEH, nearly 600 occurred in rural Mayan

---

51. Ibid., 1: 86, 107.

communities between late 1981 and 1983. In the majority of massacres, the CEH found "evidence of multiple ferocious acts preceding, during, and after the killing of the victims. The assassination of children, often by beating them against the wall or by throwing them alive into graves to be later crushed by the bodies of dead adults; amputation of limbs; impaling victims; pouring gasoline on people and burning them alive; extraction of organs; removal of fetuses from pregnant women ... the military destroyed ceremonial sites, sacred places, and cultural symbols. Indigenous language and dress were repressed."[52] In some departments, soldiers drove upward of 80 percent of the population from their homes, breaking the highland's agricultural cycle, leading to hunger and widespread deprivation. *Memoria del silencio* depicted this campaign, which it ruled to be genocidal, not as state decomposition but state formation, a carefully calibrated stage in the military's plan to establish national stability through an incorporation of Mayan peasants into government institutions and a return to constitutional rule.[53]

A willingness to employ historical methodology and make historical judgments allowed the commission to examine the racist fury that underwrote this killing not as an unchanging value but as one element of a dominant, elastic ideology radicalized by the circumstances of war. The CEH was particularly interested in the strategic thinking of a group of young, modernizing military officers who, beginning in the late 1970s, increasingly identified the kind of chaos that plagued Guatemala as an obstacle to national security. The strength of the insurgency, the officers concluded, could not simply be blamed on communism but rather on social "problems that

---

52. Ibid., 5: 43.
53. Ibid., 4: 75.

have very long and deep roots in the social system."[54] They
began to sketch out a doctrine that sought to achieve national
security through nation building. Codified in a National Plan
of Security and Development and executed through sequential
campaign policy papers, the doctrine, which the CEH dubbed
"strategic democracy," represented a breakthrough for an
army that had long served as the corrupt private gendarme
of the landed oligarchy.[55] Its short-term goals included the
temporary suspension of indiscriminate urban death squad
violence, improvement in the administrative functions of the
government, and an anti-corruption campaign—all designed
to increase the legitimacy of the state. Long-term objectives
(all achieved by the time the military agreed to negotiate an
end to the war) entailed convening a constituent assembly,
adopting a new constitution, presidential elections, demilita-
rization of certain state agencies, and normalization of diplomatic relations, which in many instances had been suspended
in reaction to government repression.

The first step in implementing such a project was to destroy
the insurgency. In late 1981, army detachments moved into the
Western Highlands and initiated a campaign of massacres
and executions in Mayan communities, identified by the army
as the support base of the rebels. Campaign plans analyzed
by the CEH identified the integration of indigenous communities into government institutions as a primary counterinsurgent objective. Military strategists focused on what they
identified as the "closed," caste-like isolation of Mayans as the
reason for their supposed collective susceptibility to communism: "the existence of diverse ethnic groups, with different
languages and dialects demonstrates the partial nature of

---

54. Ibid., 1: 198–99.
55. Ibid., 1: 188–201; 3: 321–25.

national integration due to a lack of a common identity."
Mayans, said a 1982 military policy paper, "have joined the
guerrilla due to a lack of communication with the state."[56]
The National Plan of Security and Development called for
nationalism to be "disseminated in the countryside," particularly through a literacy campaign that would make Indians
more "susceptible" to "new ideas."[57] Another 1982 action plan
called for the establishment of a "spirit of nationalism and the
creation of channels of participation and integration for the
different ethnic groups that make up our nationality."[58] To
these strategic considerations, the CEH argued, officers added
racialist fears, amplified by Guatemala's apartheid-like social
system, about Mayans: that they were susceptible to manipulation by outsiders, for example, or that their participation
in the insurgency was driven by an "atavistic" desire to take
revenge for centuries of abuse.

A historicized understanding of the relationship between
ideas and actions led the CEH to rule that the military,
between 1981 and 1983, had committed "acts of genocide."
Genocide is a notoriously difficult crime to prove. Its collective nature—the need to establish that perpetrators were
driven by hatred of a targeted group and acted in concert to
"destroy in whole or in part" that group—means, as legal
theorist William Schabas writes, "evidence of hateful motive
[is] an integral part of the proof of existence of a genocidal
plan, and therefore of genocidal intent." But the introduction of "motive" as a probative requirement is daunting, for
where the "defence can raise a doubt about the existence of
a motive, it will have cast a large shadow of uncertainty as

56. Ibid., 3: 322.
57. Ibid., 1: 98.
58. Ibid., 3: 323.

to the existence of genocidal intent."[59] Yet racism, or "hatred of the group" as Schabas puts it, is a historical category, and efforts to present it not as such but as a stable, isolated value open the door to exculpation based on historical justification. In Guatemala, for example, government officials refused to accept the CEH's conclusion that the state committed genocide against Mayans, instead arguing that the military acted in defense of national security. Guatemalan president Alvaro Arzú Irigoyen dismissed the CEH's ruling, stating that "genocide is the desire to exterminate an ethnic group, and this was not the cause of the conflict."[60] The CEH's turn to history allowed it to reject such a defense. Rather than arguing that racism is a certain manifestation of a determinative eliminationist ideology and psychology (an argument difficult, in any context, to sustain) the commission instead examined how racism came to be deeply embedded in state structures and discourses over time, in relation to land distribution, labor practices, and political struggles. The imperatives of war, both civil and class, accelerated nationalism, anti-communism, and racism into a murderous fusion: as a "contextual ideological element," *Memoria del silencio* writes, racism allowed the army to equate Indians with the insurgents and generated the belief that they were "distinct, inferior, a little less than human and removed from the moral universe of the perpetrators, making their elimination less problematic."[61]

Discussion about the efficacy of truth commissions often confuses the task of commissions to document and interpret

---

59.   William A. Schabas, *Genocide in International Law: The Crimes of Crimes* (Cambridge, 2000), 254–55.

60.   *El Periódico* (Guatemala) July 1, 1999.

61.   CEH, *Memoria del silencio*, 3: 325.

acts of political violence with their function in promoting nationalism and consolidating state legitimacy.[62] Debates between critics and celebrants often turn on the proper balance between the pursuit of justice through prosecution of human rights violators and the need to establish national unity through a cathartic process of testimony, forgiveness, and reconciliation. Proponents of the latter position emphasize the therapeutic benefits of public confession, both for victims and perpetrators. "The chance to tell one's story and be heard without interruption or skepticism is crucial to so many people, and nowhere more vital than for survivors of trauma," writes legal theorist Martha Minow, as is the "commitment to produce a coherent, if complex, narrative about the entire nation's trauma."[63] Skeptics, however, either question the suitability of applying psychoanalytical concepts to political and social relations or argue that the best way to cultivate patience for proceduralism is through trials that hold perpetrators accountable.[64] This debate has been vigorous in South Africa, where the Truth and Reconciliation Commission (TRC), in contrast to the powerlessness of most other truth commissions, wielded both moral and legal

---

62. As such, they replicate what Manu Goswami has identified as an operating assumption that handicaps many studies of nationalism: they mistake categories of analysis with categories of practice. Goswami, "Rethinking the Modular Nation Form: Toward a Sociohistorical Conception of Nationalism," *Comparative Studies in Society and History* 44, no. 4 (2002): 770–99.

63. Martha Minow, *Between Vengeance and Forgiveness: Facing History after Genocide and Mass Violence* (Boston, 1998), 58.

64. Stephan Landsman, "Alternative Responses to Serious Human Rights Abuses: Of Prosecution and Truth Commissions," *Law and Contemporary Problems* 59, no. 4 (1996): 81–92.

authority yet often decided, in principle, to use the language of forgiveness and the practice of amnesty to advance national harmony. Commissioners Alex Boraine and Desmond Tutu have defended this approach, suggesting that it could serve as model for crisis regions around the globe.[65] But others describe the work of South Africa's TRC as a lost opportunity. Richard Wilson argues that its interpretation of political violence through a narrative of struggle and liberation, tempered with a Christian ethos that demanded an abandonment of vengeance for the sake of reconciliation, undermined the establishment of liberal jurisprudence. An uncompromising language of compromise failed to take seriously popular demands for justice, to move a desire for revenge toward an acceptance of proportional retribution, thus greatly delegitimizing the concept of human rights in the eyes of many, often the most marginalized, South Africans and contributing to the pursuit of extralegal forms of rough justice.[66]

Such arguments, even those from the skeptical side of the aisle (but see Richard Wilson for an exception), avoid a more rigorous analysis of the role of truth commissions as agents of nationalism. The merits of values such as national harmony and reconciliation are assumed rather than examined, reproducing the ideological work carried out by truth commissions and leaving that work unquestioned. Truth commissions, as we have seen in Argentina and Chile, perform an indispensable task in the establishment of polities. Since violence is always present in the founding and preservation of political societies, the trick

---

65.   Alex Boraine, *A Country Unmasked* (Oxford, 2000); Desmond Tutu, *No Future without Forgiveness* (New York, 1999).

66.   Richard A. Wilson, *The Politics of Truth and Reconciliation in South Africa: Legitimizing the Post-Apartheid State* (Cambridge, 2001).

of nationalism is to turn that violence into, as Hannah Arendt put it, "cogent metaphors or universally applicable tales."[67] Truth commissions sequester the "violence of foundation"— transmuting the atrocities of military regimes into touchstones on which to affirm a new liberal order—while concealing the "violence of conservation" that maintains that order, which in the cases discussed here means the ongoing power and impunity of the military.[68] In Chile, as we saw, the Comisión Nacional de Verdad y Reconciliación, forced to deal more directly with the past than its immediate Argentine predecessor, mythologized the coup that brought Pinochet to power as a regrettable yet necessary measure needed to prevent national ruin.

Carlos Nino and Jaime Malamud-Goti consciously offered a notion of political violence decontextualized from all but the most hazy history and social relations, with a valuation of liberal morals transcendent of those relations. Yet they knew that for those values to have force and legitimacy, they would have to be reinforced by some measure of retributive justice. The reality of political power in which subsequent truth commissions operated, not just in Chile and Guatemala but in Uruguay, El Salvador, and Peru as well, broke this link, leading to what Nino described as a "second-best" option: commissions and no trials.[69] Yet subsequent Argentine and

---

67. Hannah Arendt, *On Revolution* (New York, 1963), 20.

68. Arno J. Mayer, *The Furies: Violence and Terror in the French and Russian Revolutions* (Princeton, NJ, 2000), 75.

69. Nino, *Radical Evil*, 146. Hayner, *Unspeakable Truths*, 38–40, 53–54, describes the work of commissions in Uruguay and El Salvador. For Peru, which presented its findings in August 2003 and in many ways is not comparable to the commissions here under examination due to the particular nature of insurgent and state violence, see cverdad.org.pe.

Chilean history suggests that the fortification of liberal institutions and norms has indeed come about through the pursuit of criminal justice, both in national and international court systems, affirming Nino and Malamud-Goti's original insight. Human rights groups in both countries, made up largely of victims and their relatives, have refused to allow truth commissions to put "paid" on the debate over the past. They have instead waged an ongoing battle for some degree of legal accountability, astutely appealing for international help in pressing their case. Pinochet's 1998 arrest in London and the subsequent attempts to extradite him to Spain—while occasioning a reaction on the right—have sparked a revitalization of Chile's legal system. In the wake of the dictator's capture, human rights advocates have creatively circumvented his amnesty law, arguing that, since no corpses have been recovered, political disappearances are ongoing crimes and hence not protected by the amnesty.[70] Courts have recently convicted a number of officers, while hundreds more face trial. In addition, some fourteen years after Chile's transit to democracy, the state, in response to ongoing demands by the victims of torture during the dictatorship, has convened a Comisión Nacional sobre la Detención Política y la Tortura, which received testimony from more than 35,000 Chileans whose experiences, because they survived their detention, were not documented in the previous Truth and Reconciliation commission, which addressed only disappearances, political executions, and torture leading to death. It is anticipated that the new commission's conclusions will offer a far more damning interpretation of the military's actions than that provided

---

70. Sebastian Brett, ed., *When Tyrants Tremble: The Pinochet Case* (New York, 1999); Roger Burbach, *The Pinochet Affair: State Terrorism and Global Justice* (New York, 2003).

by its predecessor.[71] In Argentina, the recent repeal of the "full stop" and other amnesty laws, likewise in response to pressure from political groups, has reopened legal investigations into rights violations committed during the "dirty war."[72]

In Guatemala, state terror was so brutal, so successful in destroying political opposition, that it shattered the conceit that future social solidarity could be constructed from a description of past human rights transgressions or the supposed collective healing that comes from telling one's story to an official body, leading the CEH to break with past commissions and present violence not just in descriptive or moral terms but in historical and social science ones as well. This methodological innovation, in turn, allowed the commission to rule that the military committed acts of genocide, for genocide is, by definition, a collective crime and, as such, demands social and historical analysis. This was particularly true in the case of Guatemala, where the imperatives of counterinsurgent state formation melded seamlessly with a racism politicized by anti-communism. Rather than dissolving moral or legal responsibility in a larger structural solution, as Argentine and Chilean jurists feared it would, the CEH's historical interpretation both unearthed the racist premises that motivated the 1981–1983 scorched-earth campaign and provided support for the elaboration of a set of policy recommendations that sought to prevent the reoccurrence of political violence through the creation of a more equitable society. It called for the adoption of a progressive tax system, increased state spending on human needs, a dismantling of the repressive intelligence apparatus,

71. "Documento de Cheyre se anticipa a duro informe sobre la tortura," *La Tercera*, November 6, 2004.

72. Human Rights Watch, Monthly Update, "Argentina Faces Its Past," August 2003, hrw.org.

along with the implementation of unfulfilled political, legal, and economic reforms agreed to, but not implemented, in the peace accords. Attention to structural analysis and causal history also allowed the CEH to avoid constituting itself as an unreflective instrument of nation building. Unlike commissions in Argentina and Chile, it acknowledged that the roots of the violence lay in the clash between those who fought for a more equitable society and those who defended, with increasing viciousness, the established order. It also refused to draw too clear a line between a past marred by unspecified intolerance and a contemporary polity based on pluralism and proceduralism. The implication, of course, is that the new constitutional order the CEH sought to fortify was an extension of the counterinsurgency.

Some would argue that this is too much knowledge, that in a country such as Guatemala, where democracy enjoys but a tenuous hold and the conflicts of the past continue into the present, to overexpose history is to court disaster. *Memoria del silencio* could be criticized for focusing too much on institutional and historical analysis, on not devoting enough of its energy to exploring the ethnographic or psychological dimensions of terror, or how violence was experienced by individuals and communities. Such an approach would have aligned the CEH more closely with what many say should be the primary task of truth commissions: the promotion of individual and collective healing to bring about national cohesion.[73]

Yet preliminary evidence suggests it was just the commission's epistemological certainty that, even while exposing divisions, has reinforced those organizations that work to strengthen the rule and value of law. The CEH presented

---

73. See Minow, *Between Vengeance and Forgiveness*, 61–90.

its findings in Guatemala's National Theater in early 1999 to a front row of military and government officials and an overflowing crowd made up of victims, their relatives, and members of human rights and Mayan organizations, many of whom were survivors of political movements decimated by state repression. Chief Commissioner Christian Tomuschat summarized the CEH's conclusions. While he condemned violations committed by the Left and criticized Cuba for supporting the rebels, his remarks, backed up by overwhelming statistical evidence, left little doubt as to responsibility: "the magnitude and irrational inhumanity of the violence . . . cannot be understood as a consequence of a confrontation between two armed parties" but rather of the "structure and nature" of Guatemalan society; the US government and US corporations acted to "maintain Guatemala's archaic and unjust socio-economic system"; the army carried out a "blind anticommunist crusade, without regard to a single juridical principle or the most basic ethical or religious values, resulting in a loss of all human morality."[74] The audience greeted the speech with tears and deafening applause.[75] The cathartic power of the event rested not in the elision of social division and political struggle through an avoidance of history and appeals to forgiveness but rather in their accentuation: Guatemala's president refused to climb the stage to accept the report, sitting instead, along with government officials and military officers, in stunned silence. A few days later, the US ambassador dismissed charges of Washington's complicity; it was "better," he said, "to focus on the future and not

---

74. "Palabras del Sr. Christian Tomuschat, Coordinador de la CEH en ocasión de la entrega del informe de la Comisión para el Esclarecimiento Histórico," Guatemala City, February 25, 1999.
75. Tomuschat, "Clarification Commission in Guatemala."

the past."[76] Over the last four years, successive governments have ignored the CEH's findings and recommendations while human rights groups, initially dismissive of the commission's enabling mandate, have claimed its final report as their own. As in Argentina and Chile, these groups have helped strengthen the rule of law through rare legal victories in the country's shaky criminal system, often citing *Memoria del silencio* as contextual evidence.[77]

Following other truth commissions, the Comisión para el Esclarecimiento Histórico used a variety of methods to approach the past, resulting in a twelve-volume report weighted with statistical charts and analyses, pages upon pages of victims' names, typologies of violations, and lengthy and opaque discussions of national and international jurisprudence. But its influence and legacy resides in the confidence and lucidity of its historical conclusions. Such interpretive certainty has not, contrary to the fears of transitional-justice intellectuals, ended the debate over Guatemala's past but rather reinforced, however tentatively, those fighting to define its future.[78]

*

---

76.   CERIGUA News Wire, Weekly Briefs, March 4, 1999.

77.   Charles Hale et al. "Democracy as Subterfuge: Researchers under Siege in Guatemala," *LASA Forum* 33, no. 3 (Fall 2002): 6–10.

78.   Elizabeth Oglesby's study of the short- and long-term impact of the CEH argues that the report did not "fix" a particular "version of history, but rather [established] some parameters within which future discussions can take place. In a context like Guatemala, where until recently it was extremely dangerous to raise the issue of human rights violations in a public venue, this means establishing some firm ground, the Truth Commission report is out there with the imprimatur of the United Nations, it's impossible now to deny certain realities." Yet Oglesby points out that the interpretation of those realities is still debatable. For

instance, the project funded by the US Agency of International Development to disseminate a summary of the report omits any mention of the United States' role in the violence, including the CIA's actions in 1954, and ignores the report's structural analysis, instead portraying the violence as the by-product of armed struggle—a clear contradiction of the CEH's conclusions. Oglesby, "The Truth Commission and Teaching History in Guatemala," paper presented at Carnegie Council History and the Politics of Reconciliation Workshop, University of British Columbia, Vancouver, November 8, 2003.

CHAPTER TWO

Judging Genocide: The Reasoning Behind the Truth Commission's Ruling

For a small country, Guatemala has had an impressive history. Its 1944 October Revolution was one of the first efforts in Latin America to try to make good on the social democratic promise offered by the Allied victory in World War II. In 1954 it had the unfortunate distinction to suffer the first Latin American Cold War coup. That US-sponsored event, in turn, led to two important consequences: throughout the rest of his life, Che Guevara, who was in Guatemala at the time, cited the intervention as a key moment in his political radicalization, and the United States, seven years later, would try to replicate its Guatemalan success in Cuba with the Bay of Pigs intervention. In the 1960s, following the Cuban Revolution, Guatemala was one of the first Latin American countries to develop both a socialist insurgency *and* an anti-communist counterinsurgency. Practices the United States rehearsed in Guatemala would be applied throughout Latin America in the coming decades.[1] In the 1980s, the final escalation of the superpower conflict turned Guatemala, along with Nicaragua and El Salvador, into one of the Cold War's final battlefields.

In February 1999 the United Nations-administered

---

1. Martha K. Huggins, *Political Policing: The United States and Latin America* (Durham, NC, 1998).

Historical Clarification Commission (CEH) released the results of its investigation into the political repression that underwrote this history. The commission not only ruled that the state bore overwhelming responsibility for more than 200,000 political murders but that during a particularly brutal period between 1981 and 1983 it had committed acts of genocide against its Mayan population, who make up 60 percent of a population of 10 million people. The CEH also condemned both the United States government for financially, technically, and materially supporting Guatemalan security forces and US businesses for "maintaining archaic and unjust social and economic relations."[2]

These forceful conclusions, uncharacteristic of the usually conciliatory tone of truth commissions, were made possible by the CEH's unique use of historical analysis and narrative. Despite the fact that they exercised no power to indict, prosecute, or punish, past truth commissions in Argentina, Chile, and El Salvador focused primarily on a juridical interpretation of human rights violations—inquiries that judged individual transgressions in light of national and international legal doctrine, limiting themselves to asking "who did what to whom and how." Other than providing hazy descriptions of political polarization, these commissions studiously avoided asking why repression took place. Confronted with the inability of liberal jurisprudence to represent adequately the horrors of a four-decade civil war, the CEH broke with past Latin American commissions and placed human rights violations at the end of a historical narrative that in effect begins with

---

2. See the summary by Christian Tomuschat, the CEH's president, given at the presentation of the report.

the Spanish conquest.[3] Yet rather than dilute institutional responsibility (the commission was prohibited from identifying individual violators) in abstract structural causes, the CEH joined historical and juridical analysis in a manner that strengthened legal doctrine. The application of history to law allowed the commission to rule that the Guatemalan state committed acts of genocide against its Mayan population, for genocide, while defined by intent—a psychological state most comfortably fitted to individuals—is always a social crime, collective in execution and consequence.

A state racist in theory and practice

The CEH was established in a series of United Nations-brokered agreements between the military and rebels that in 1996 ended one of the longest and most bloody civil conflicts in the world. Like other accords negotiated by an enervated guerrilla leadership and a victorious military, it angered national and international human rights organizations. The CEH did not have the power to subpoena witnesses or records and its final report could not "individualize responsibility" or have "legal effects."[4] The agreement, however, in a strategic avoidance of potentially deal-breaking specifics, left vague other aspects of the commission's work. Unlike the strict mandates of the Argentine and Chilean truth commissions,

---

3. I discuss some of the ethical questions raised by the CEH's historical methodology in Greg Grandin, "Chronicles of a Guatemalan Genocide Foretold: Violence, Trauma, and the Limits of Historical Inquiry," *Nepantla* 1, no. 2 (2000): 391–412.

4. The accord is in the commission's final report. Comisión para el Esclarecimiento Histórico (CEH), *Guatemala: Memoria del silencio*, 12 vols. (Guatemala City, 1999), 1:23–26. The report is available online at hrdata.aaas.org.

which limited the time period and violations to be investigated, the CEH accord did not define the crimes to be examined, the period to be considered, or the commission's methodology.

A number of factors led the commission—comprised of German human rights law expert Christian Tomuschat, and Guatemalans Otilia Lux de Cotí, a Mayan educator, and Alfredo Balsells, another law professor—to apply a more critical historical method than did previous commissions. The duration and brutality of the violence, an unrepentant military and oligarchy, an indifferent state, and profound social and racial cleavages undercut the argument that future deterrence could be brought about by an affirmation of shared social values—an argument usually made to support a more open-ended historical interpretation of the causes of human rights violations. The ambiguity of the accord allowed the commissioners to interpret its mandate broadly:

> To address the historical causes of this most tragic epoch ... implies dealing with conditions that developed over time and whose effects have accumulated influence on human conduct and social practice ... Guatemalan history chronicles manifold, enduring forms of violence that affect segments of the population. This violence is clearly reflected in political life, in social relations, and in the realm of work, and its origins are of an economic, political, ideological, religious, and ethnic character.[5]

Based on the collection of over 8,000 testimonies from victims and their relatives, the CEH concluded that the state was responsible for 93 percent of the violations and that the military committed 626 massacres. The guerrillas were

---

5. Ibid., 82.

assigned responsibility for 3 percent of the violations and 32 collective killings. During the course of the conflict, the military and its allied agents killed or "disappeared" over 200,000 Guatemalans. Yet *Memoria del silencio*, as the final report is titled, goes well beyond divvying out responsibility for the violence to the state and the guerrillas. Starting with an introduction that lays out staggering statistical evidence of social inequality—the country's health, education, literacy, and nutritional indicators are among the most unjust in the world despite an abundance of national wealth—the CEH spends the rest of its first volume chronicling the "causes and origins" of Guatemala's armed conflict. It is a damning account that indicts not just the nation's ruling elite but its culture and history as well.

The CEH focuses a good part of its analysis on the political intolerance brought about by a deterioration of liberal state institutions. A weak state could not fulfill even the most rudimentary redistributionist function, which contributed to a "political culture where intolerance defined the totality of social interaction."[6] Yet in contrast to past truth commission reports, the CEH describes intolerance and polarization as effects, not wellsprings, of social relations and political actions. Nor, despite its harsh criticisms of the United States, does it attempt to displace blame onto the foreign powers:

> [I]t is not possible to present simple explanations that present the armed conflict as a manifestation of the Cold War confrontation between the East and the West . . . If the most visible actors of the conflict were the military and the insurgency, the historical investigation conducted by the CEH provides evidence of the responsibility and participation, in different forms, of segments

---

6. Ibid., 79.

of the economic elite, political parties, and diverse sectors of civil society ... In this sense, any reduction [of the conflict] to the logic of two actors is not only insufficient, but misleading.[7]

The CEH identifies three mutually dependent "structural" or "historical" causes of state violence: economic exclusion, racism, and political authoritarianism. Its analysis rests heavily on "theories of authoritarianism," elaborated by southern cone social scientists, that see Cold War military regimes as emerging from a particular path of dependent economic development.[8] Yet while these explanations tend toward abstraction, the CEH carefully unfolds its narrative in close chronology, particularly in its description of Guatemala's post-1954 history. The transition to coffee cultivation at the end of the nineteenth century intensified colonial exploitation, racism, and authoritarianism. Guatemala's plantation elites gobbled up vast amounts of land and came to rely on the state—"racist in theory and practice"—to ensure the cheap supply of labor, mostly Mayans from highland communities. A series of forced labor laws combined with land loss to "increase the economic subordination" of Mayans and

---

7. Ibid., 80.

8. See, e.g., Guillermo O'Donnell, *Modernization and Bureaucratic-Authoritarianism* (Berkeley, 1973), and "Tensions in the Bureaucratic-Authoritarian State and the Question of Democracy," in David Collier (ed.), *The New Authoritarianism in Latin America* (Princeton, 1979), and Fernando Henrique Cardoso, *Autoritrismo e democratizaç o* (Rio de Janeiro, 1975). See also the essays in Kees Koonings and Dirk Kruijt (eds.), *Societies of Fear: The Legacy of Civil War, Violence and Terror in Latin America* (London, 1999). See Idelber Avelar's important discussion on these theories in *The Untimely Present: Postdictatorial Latin American Fiction and the Task of Mourning* (Durham, NC, 1999), Chapter 2.

poor ladinos (Guatemalans not considered Mayan). This model of coercive development in turn militarized the state, which focused its energies on enforcing policies, particularly the acquisition of labor through debt and vagrancy laws, that benefited the coffee oligarchy.[9] Since the end of the nineteenth century, "the landed class," writes the CEH, "especially the sector connected to the cultivation of coffee . . . imposed its economic interests on the state and society."[10]

The CEH identifies political actions taken either in response to social exploitation or in defense of entrenched interests as the mainspring of the Guatemalan conflict: 'state violence has been fundamentally aimed against the excluded, the poor, and the Maya, as well as those who struggled in favor of just and more equitable society . . . Thus a vicious circle was created in which social injustice led to protest and subsequently to political instability, to which there were always only two responses: repression or military coups."[11] Confronted with movements demanding "economic, political, social, or cultural change, the state increasingly resorted to violence and terror in order to maintain social control. Political violence was thus a direct expression of structural violence."[12]

This dynamic eased and even reversed for a ten-year period when, following a democratic revolution in 1944, two

---

9. Many historians share this assessment. For Guatemala, see David McCreery, *Rural Guatemala, 1760–1940* (Stanford, 1994). For Guatemala's transition to export capitalism compared with Mexico, see Alan Knight, "Debt Bondage in Latin America," in Leonie Archer (ed.), *Slavery and Other Forms of Unfree Labour* (New York, 1989).

10. CEH, *Guatemala: Memoria del silencio*, 1:81.

11. Ibid., 5:21–22.

12. Ibid.

reformist administrations curtailed many of the prerogatives and privileges of the coffee oligarchy. The CEH identifies this period as an "immediate antecedent" for the civil war. The new governments ratified a social democratic constitution, ended forced labor, legalized unions, enacted a labor code, expanded the vote, and passed a far-reaching land reform. These measures "increased ideological polarization and internal political struggle within an international context that was increasingly charged by the tensions of the east-west struggle."[13] An "archaic judicial structure" that could not deal with the conflicts generated by the rapid expansion of new rights, including those granted by the land and labor reforms, aggravated social tensions and deepened polarization. While the "defenders of the established order" quickly mobilized against the state, opposition came from other sectors as well.[14] Rural peasant and indigenous mobilization along with the legalization and growing influence of the Communist Party reinforced an anti-communism that had deep roots among the middle class, Catholic Church, and military. In turn, resistance to reform both radicalized and divided revolutionary parties.

This democratic decade, according to the CEH, "awoke the energies and hopes" of Guatemalans who had "yearned to overcome the past." This awakening took place in a larger global context in which "the world was entering a new political period with the defeat of fascism and the promise offered by capitalist economic development." The CEH describes the US-orchestrated 1954 counter-revolution as a national "trauma" that had a "collective political effect" on a generation of young, reform-minded Guatemalans: "so drastic was

13. Ibid., 1:100.
14. Ibid., 103–5.

the closing of channels of participation and so extensive was the recourse to violence that it is considered one of the factors that led to the guerrilla insurgency of 1960."[15] Expectations raised and struggles fought during this period resonated throughout Guatemala's subsequent civil war. In the countryside, many of the land conflicts that fueled peasant participation in political movements and the insurgency date back to the Arbenz land reform of 1953.

The US intervention reinitiated the "exclusivist dynamic." The state once again put "itself at the bidding of a minority at the expense of the majority."[16] It also led to two new consequences important to understanding the development of Cold War political violence. First, Cold War tensions and anti-communism energized nationalist racism and reinvigorated old forms and justifications of domination. A racially divided and economically stratified Guatemala was a tinderbox; counterinsurgent fear was the match. "What happened during the period of armed conflict," writes the CEH, "can be summed up as a process by which the radius of exclusion and the notion of an internal enemy" was extended and intensified through the whole of society.[17] Second, the Cold War radically transformed the possibilities of political alliances. In the past, the state responded to demands made by political movements not only with repression but with concessions and negotiations as well. The triumph of the 1944 revolution was the high point of this pattern. Following 1954 and intensifying after the 1959 Cuban Revolution, Guatemalan elites increasingly turned to the United States in order to confront domestic threats to their power. The

---

15. Ibid., 107.
16. Ibid., 86.
17. Ibid., 83.

balance tipped in the state's favor and repression gave way to full-scale terror.

Counterinsurgent motives, genocidal intent

The CEH's marriage of history and law was more than one of convenience. Beyond providing a fulsome description of the conditions that give rise to political terror, the CEH's historical method proved indispensable to its ruling on genocide, a difficult crime to define under liberal jurisprudence. Most recent attempts to judge cases of genocide use the definition established by the 1948 United Nations Convention on the Prevention and Punishment of the Crime of Genocide, which defines genocide as one of a series of acts committed with the "intent to destroy, in whole or in part, a national, ethnical, racial, or religious group, as such."[18] While genocide is defined by intent—a psychological state associated with an individual—its collective nature challenges the very premise by which intent is defined.

Intent can be defined two ways. Specific intent attaches to "perpetrators whose actual aim or purpose is to realize

---

18. Convention on the Prevention and Punishment of the Crime of Genocide, December 9, 1948, 102 Stat. 3045, 78 U.N.T.S. 277, U.N. G.A. Res. 260, U.N. GAOR, 3d Sess., 179th plen. mtg. at 174, U.N. Doc. A/810 (1948). The recently adopted Rome Statute of the International Criminal Court, the body that will, if instituted, judge future cases of genocide, adopted the following definition of intent: "[A] person has intent where a) In relation to conduct, that person means to engage in the conduct; b) In relation to consequence, that person means to cause that consequence or is aware that it will occur in the ordinary course of events." See Mahnoush H. Arsanjani, "The Rome Statute of the International Criminal Court," *American Journal of International Law* 93, no. 1 (1999): 22.

certain forbidden consequences." General intent describes the state of mind governing the actions of individuals who "knew to a practical certainty what the consequences of those actions would be, regardless of whether or not they deliberately sought to realize those consequences." In the first case, the act is committed with the *purpose* that the consequence would occur. In the second, it is the *knowledge* that a particular act would have a certain consequence.[19] In the formulation "x killed y because x was jealous," *intent* is used to describe the psychological state of whether x knew that his or her actions would lead to the death of y, whereas *motive* is used to describe the reason, jealousy, for the actions. In most cases, the relationship between motive and intent is corroborative, that is, unveiling the motive makes more certain a charge that an individual intended a particular act. In legal proceedings, motive is usually always supplementary, whereas intent is essential in establishing guilt.[20] The separation between motive and intent is a juridical artifice, used to cull out responsibility for a particular act from a larger historical sequence of action and meaning. Liberal jurisprudence, of

19. Alexander K. A. Greenawalt, "Rethinking Genocidal Intent: The Case for a Knowledge-Based Interpretation," *Columbia Law Review* (December 1999): 2266.

20. Consider this distinction between motive and intent found in a standard law text: "Intent relates to the means and motive to the ends, but . . . where the end is the means to yet another end, then the medial end may also be considered in terms of intent. Thus, when A breaks into B's house in order to get money to pay his debts, it is appropriate to characterize the purpose of taking money as the intent and the desire to pay his debts as the motive." Wayne R. LaFave and Austin W. Scott Jr., *Criminal Law*, 2nd ed. (St. Paul, 1986), 228, cited in Greenawalt, "Rethinking Genocidal Intent."

course, recognizes that individuals, actions, and psychological
states exist within a larger constellation of moral and political
relations and over the course of time has produced a series of
doctrines to account for a diffusion of responsibility and still
retain the authority to punish a given act. Crimes committed
by more than one person or as a result of a chain of command
and actions taken in pursuit of a greater good—either in self-
or social defense—are all defined and judged accordingly.

Genocide, however, poses a challenge to liberal jurisprudence to address collective crimes, for it is collective in two
ways. First, the victim category is not simply a group of individuals but rather a racial, religious, or ethnic group. Second,
it would often be practically impossible to conclude an act
was committed with genocidal intent by an examination of
an isolated act.[21] In order to establish that a particular act was
committed with genocidal intent, that is, in order to prove that
the perpetrators had either knowledge or purpose that their
actions would result in the destruction in whole or in part of
a defined group, it is perhaps essential, not just corroborative,
to establish motive. Motive both links individual acts within
a larger campaign and furthers an argument that the victims
were understood in racial or ethnic terms.

Yet the introduction of motive as a probative requirement
undermines the very definition of genocide. Just as lawyers
often fear an appeal to history will be used to exonerate individuals from the consequences of their actions, a search for
motive can dilute the racial content of a crime, *for race is never
just race*. Racial, ethnic, and religious identity intertwine in all
aspects of social life and national history. The motives that
drive genocidal campaigns may not be understood in racial
terms at all or may be justified in terms that emphasize a

---

21. Except perhaps in the case of Hiroshima or Nagasaki.

greater good. This is true even in a case as extreme as the Jewish Holocaust, the historical standard on which rest commonsensical understandings of genocide. In no other genocidal event, it seems, has motive mapped onto intent as seamlessly as it did during the Holocaust. The Nazis intended to destroy Jews because they were Jews. But even in this case, debate inevitably arises when historians attempt to situate intent within a larger array of social, political, and economic relations. Was Nazi intent to eliminate Jews a reaction to being pushed back on the Eastern Front? What was its relationship to other ideological motivations—to nationalism or anti-communism? Were genocidal acts committed to establish an emotional bond with the Führer? What is the relationship between those who executed and those who ordered genocidal acts?[22]

In the Guatemalan case, the question that confronted the CEH was this: despite the massive violence visited upon indigenous communities by the military between 1981 and 1983, were Mayans killed because they were Mayan, or because they represented the real or perceived support base of the insurgency? The fact that the army did not inflict the same terror on indigenous communities that did not support the rebels lent weight to the claim that the violence was not genocidal but rather counterinsurgent. Indeed, Guatemalan president Alvaro Arzú rejected the CEH's genocide ruling in such terms: "I do not believe that this macabre episode of thirty-six years was genocide. Genocide is the desire to exterminate an ethnic group, a race, and this was not the reason for this

---

22. Ron Rosenbaum, *Explaining Hitler: The Search for the Origins of His Evil* (New York, 1998), and Christopher R. Browning, *Fateful Months: Essays on the Emergence of the Final Solution* (New York, 1985).

brutal conflict."[23] From the same assumptions, many on the Left who were members of the insurgency or affiliated social movements were uncomfortable with the charge of genocide. For them, the description of the repression as genocide risked overshadowing the fact that the state was being challenged by a powerful, multiethnic coalition demanding economic and political reform. Many felt that by purportedly denying indigenous participation in the popular movement, the claim of genocide risked reducing the history of the repression to a simplified tale of ladino violence heaped on defenseless Indians.

The CEH avoided this dilemma by carefully interpreting the UN's convention on genocide to differentiate motive from intent. "It is important to distinguish," wrote the CEH, "between 'the *intent* to destroy [a group], in whole or in part' . . . from the motives for such intention. In order to rule genocide, the intention to destroy the group is enough, whatever be the motives. For example, if the motive to intend to kill an ethnic group is not racist, but military, the crime is still genocide."[24] Once it made this foray into a more historically

---

23. *El Periódico*, June 30, 1999, 3.

24. CEH, *Guatemala: Memoria del silencio*, 3:316. A review of the history of the drafting of the convention confirms the CEH's distinction between intent and motive. The Soviet delegate attempted to insert language that would make "the qualifying fact" of genocide "not simply the destruction of certain groups but destruction for the reason that the people in them belonged to a given race or nationality, or had specific religious beliefs." The majority of delegates, however, rejected such a definition on the grounds that such wording would too narrowly limit the definition's application. The Siamese delegate, for instance, voted for the convention because it did not specifically define motives. See the discussion in Greenawalt, "Rethinking Genocidal Intent."

grounded understanding of genocide—unavoidable considering the development of events under consideration—the CEH had to contend with the potential for the consideration of motive to exonerate the perpetrators. The repressive state *was* threatened by a powerful insurgency. Mayans *did* participate in massive numbers in social movements and in the insurgency. The military *did* principally target indigenous communities that supported the guerrillas.

The CEH neutralized the potential of motive to absolve by using historical analysis to reveal the racialized assumptions of military strategy. In its "causes and origins" section, the commission described how patterns of rule and resistance developed along distinct racial lines. Unlike what occurred, for instance, in neighboring Mexico, the deepening of capitalist relations strengthened ethnic affiliation in Guatemala. In Mexico, particularly in the central valley, a vibrant colonial economy broke down indigenous ethnicity into a more homogeneous, but still racially marked, peasant identity.[25] In contrast, Guatemala's peripheral colonial and early republican economy buffered the consolidation and endurance of distinct indigenous identities centered on residential communities. With the introduction of coffee in the mid-nineteenth century, the creation of Guatemala's agrarian proletariat took place along clearly defined ethnic lines.

Guatemala's liberal coffee state was "characterized by its contradictions."[26] It eliminated the juridical distinctions between Indians and non-Indians but also abolished [corporate] social protections, such as the right to land and political

---

25. See Alan Knight, "Racism, Revolution and Indigenismo: Mexico, 1910–1940," in Richard Graham (ed.), *The Idea of Race in Latin America, 1870–1940* (Austin, 1994), 78.

26. CEH, *Guatemala: Memoria del silencio*, 1:91.

autonomy.[27] On the one hand, the state promoted assimilation into a single national identity. On the other hand, it enforced labor and tax policies that maintained Mayans as a distinct group. Mayans were singled out as obvious sources of labor and, when wages proved insufficient to attract a voluntary work force, the state enacted a series of extraeconomic "incentives" to secure workers, including forced labor drafts, debt peonage, and vagrancy laws. At times, whole communities became the captive work force of specific planters. Furthermore, unable to support a full-time labor force, coffee production relied on the ongoing existence of Indian communities to supply the subsistence needs of their seasonal workers. At the same time, Mayans used the wages they did receive to strengthen community institutions and traditions threatened by a shrinking subsistence land base due to population growth and commercial agricultural production. Guatemalan colonialism and capitalism did not create indigenous culture, but the particular form colonialism and capitalism took provided Indians space in which to survive *as* Indians.

Guatemala's nineteenth-century political trajectory likewise reinforced ethnic identity. As in Mexico, Indians and peasants allied themselves with non-indigenous political elites as their interests and identifications dictated. Unlike in Mexico, however, indigenous peasants usually supported conservative opposition to liberal reforms, which, on the whole, tended to undermine indigenous political authority and land rights. When coffee planters took control of the state and its ideological apparatus in 1871, Mayan political participation was either denied or portrayed as reactionary and ahistorical. Nationalists constantly blamed their political failures on indigenous reaction, and nearly uniformly wrote Indians

---

27. Ibid., 92.

out of their narration of national progress and destiny. The fall of the first independent liberal regime in 1838, the failure of the Central American Federation in 1840, and the endurance of a long postcolonial conservative regime (1839–71) were all blamed on Indians.[28]

The period between 1944 and 1954 saw a brief respite from this dynamic. But with the revolution's overthrow, "old forms of exploitation, of forced labor, of land appropriation against Indians and in favor of large landowners started again."[29] During the Cold War, the friend–enemy distinction that drives anti-communism easily took root in this fertile race soil: "Patterns of violence within a society tend to generalize," the CEH writes, "they are copied and imitated and defuse throughout the social body and are reproduced across generations. Racism, conscious or unconscious, is an important factor in the explanation of many of the excessive acts of violence committed during the history of Guatemala and the armed conflict. For a racist mentality, any form of indigenous mobilization brings to mind an atavistic uprising. In this way, it can be considered that racism was present in the most bloody moments of the armed conflict, when the indigenous population was punished as an enemy that needed to be vanquished."[30]

---

28. For still the best account of indigenous support of conservative movements, see Hazel Ingersoll, "The War of the Mountain: A Study in Reactionary Peasant Insurgency in Guatemala, 1837–1873," PhD thesis, George Washington University, 1972. For the ideological consequences of indigenous political participation, see Greg Grandin, *The Blood of Guatemala: A History of Race and Nation* (Durham, NC, 2000), chapters 3 and 6.

29. CEH, *Guatemala: Memoria del silencio*, 1:92.

30. Ibid., 93.

In order to prove genocide, the CEH applied its historical analysis to the logic of the military's 1981–82 scorched-
earth campaign. Officers drew on long-held assumptions
regarding indigenous culture to "single out [Maya] as the
internal enemy ... both a real and potential support base
for the guerrillas."[31] As one 1972 intelligence manual put it,
"the enemy has the same sociological traits as the inhabitants
of our highlands."[32] Guatemalan military analysts focused
on what they identified as the "closed," caste-like isolation
of highland indigenous communities as the reason for the
supposed collective susceptibility of Mayans to communism: "[T]he existence of diverse ethnic groups, with different languages and dialects, demonstrates the partial nature of
national integration due to a lack of a common identity."[33]
Mayans, wrote another military analyst, "have joined the
guerrilla due to a lack of communication with the state."[34]
To these assumptions, strategists added the ladino tendency
to interpret all indigenous political mobilization—on the rise
since the 1960s—as the product of outside manipulation.

The military's scorched-earth campaign, therefore, was
designed to respond to this caste threat. It brutally cut off
communities from the insurgency and broke down the
communal structures that military analysts identified as seed-
beds of guerrilla support. This explains the singularly savage
nature of the Guatemalan counterinsurgency, which targeted
not just individuals. In the majority of massacres, the CEH
found

---

31. Ibid., 5:49.
32. Ibid., 3:322.
33. Ibid.
34. Ibid.

evidence of multiple ferocious acts that preceded, accompanied, and followed the killing of the victims. The assassination of children, often by beating them against the wall or by throwing them alive into graves to be later crushed by the bodies of dead adults; amputation of limbs; impaling victims; pouring gasoline on people and burning them alive; extraction of organs; removal of fetuses from pregnant women ... The military destroyed ceremonial sites, sacred places, and cultural symbols. Indigenous language and dress were repressed ... Legitimate authority of the communities was destroyed.[35]

Mayans were identified as the enemy and killed *qua* Mayans, even if the *motivation* was to beat the insurgency.

Official responses to the report and the genocide charge have been disappointing. Unlike in Chile where President Patricio Aylwin formally apologized on behalf of the state for the crimes committed during the Pinochet years, the Guatemalan government has not claimed the CEH report as its own. During the official presentation of *Memoria del silencio* in Guatemala's National Theater, victims, their relatives, and members of popular and human rights organizations greeted the report's conclusions with clamorous applause. Guatemala's president, Alvaro Arzú, his close advisors, and military officers, however, appeared stunned. Arzú did not personally receive the report, instead delegating the government's secretary of peace to the stage. In the days that followed, official reactions were ambiguous at best. While the president begged for time to "read, analyze, and study in meticulous detail each and every word" before he would make an official statement (Arzú finished his term without issuing an official response), his secretary immediately reminded the press that

---

35. Ibid., 5:43.

while the work of the commission was laudable, it was important to keep in mind that "those responsible for the massacres will not be brought to justice."[36] Guatemala's minister
of defense remarked that the report was "a partial truth, since
its version of history is nothing more than the point of view
of the commission." The head of Guatemala's official tour-
ist institute complained that the report would result in more
"damage than reconciliation" because its negative portrayal
of Guatemala would cause foreign tourists to cancel their
travel plans.[37]

While the report's findings are not legally binding, *Memoria
del silencio* called for the full application of Guatemala's 1996
Law of National Reconciliation. This law allowed human
rights violators to apply for amnesty for crimes committed
during the civil war but not for acts of genocide, torture, and
forced disappearances. By ruling that aspects of the military's
1981–83 scorched-earth campaign were genocidal, the CEH
hypothetically opened the door to prosecution, calling for the
prosecution of "those crimes that the law does not exempt."[38]
It is doubtful that anyone responsible for the terror will be
charged in a national court anytime soon. In Argentina and
Chile, recent efforts to prosecute violators of human rights
in foreign courts have energized and strengthened domestic
judicial systems. In Guatemala, the first flush of defensiveness
on the part of the state tapered off into silence and neither the
government, the military, nor the oligarchy have the will or
desire to confront the past in a court of law.

---

36. Radio broadcast, *Guatemala Flash*, March 2, 1999, radio
broadcast, *Noti-7*, February 25, 1999.

37. *El Periódico*, February 26, 1999; radio broadcast, *Noti-7*,
March 2, 1999.

38. CEH, *Memoria del silencio*, 5:72.

Conclusion

Historical analysis not only supported the legal reasoning that backed the CEH's genocide ruling but provided historians with a way of distinguishing Cold War political terror from larger patterns of mobilization and repression. The CEH's analysis suggests that Mayan participation in the revolutionary movement of the 1970s and early 1980s marked a change from past indigenous strategies of dealing with the state. Through the colonial period and into the republican period, indigenous communities viewed the state as an arbiter of social relations, capable of mediating pacts, alliances, and conflicts between various social blocs.[39] Following 1954, rapid economic growth, a violent breakdown of a governing consensus among ladino elites, US intervention, and escalating state repression joined to undercut the power of indigenous elites to fulfill their role as brokers between local, regional, and national interests. Stripped of their ability to negotiate political relations, community leaders in the 1970s "confronted the state head on."[40] According to the CEH, starting in the 1970s, Mayans joined other "citizens from broad sectors of society . . . in [a] growing social mobilization and political opposition to the continuity of the country's established order."[41] The army's 1981–83 genocidal campaign can be understood in military terms as a strategic reaction to this shift in the balance governing relations of rule and resistance. In 1983, following

---

39. See the conclusion to Grandin, *Blood*, for a more detailed discussion.

40. Víctor Gálvez Borrell, Claudia Dary Fuentes, Edgar Esquit Choy, and Isabel Rodas, *¿Qué sociedad queremos? Una mirada desde el movimiento y las organizaciones mayas* (Guatemala City, 1997), 63–66.

41. CEH, *Memoria del silencio*, 5:27.

the worst of the massacres, the military quickly decentralized the responsibility of social control to civil patrols and other local institutions run by selected Mayans. In effect, this phase of the military's counterinsurgency campaign was a return to older tactics of dealing with indigenous communities. Colonial, conservative, and even liberal regimes had invested a significant amount of authority in indigenous leaders in exchange for their cooperation in administering political relations, including, when needed, pacification of unruly subjects and communities.

The CEH's innovative use of history not only distinguished motive from intent but prevented counterinsurgent justifications from mitigating the severity of the charges of military atrocities. Historical analysis explained the apparent contradiction between the particularly savage nature of the Guatemalan counterinsurgency and the fact that once the surviving Indians were perceived to be under control, once the military felt it had substituted itself for the insurgency, the killing stopped. Only history could make sense of the perverse logic of Guatemalan president General Efraín Ríos Montt's remark made at the height of the slaughter he directed: "Naturally, if a subversive operation exists in which the Indians are involved with the guerrilla, the Indians are also going to die. However, the army's philosophy is not to kill the Indians, but to win them back, to help them."[42]

---

42. Foreign Broadcast Information Service, Central America, "Rios Montt's Views on Peasant Killings, Communism," June 2, 1982.

Appendix: The Findings of the UN Commission for Historical Clarification— A State Racist in Theory and Practice

Translated by Jennifer Adair

Part one: causes and origins of the armed conflict[1]

To restore dignity to Guatemalan society, the Commission for Historical Clarification (CEH, in Spanish) seeks to promote mutual respect and encourage the observance of human rights. Guatemala is a predominantly rural country, with a majority Maya population and an overwhelmingly unjust land tenure system. Ten percent of the population controls over half of the nation's wealth, making the country the worst and most inequitable nation in terms of land distribution in all of Latin America . . . This inequality has provoked numerous conflicts over time. Concentration of economic and political power, racism and discrimination against the majority indigenous population, and economic exclusion of the poorest sectors— Maya and ladino alike—are reflected in high rates of illiteracy and the ongoing isolation of rural communities . . . No particular expertise is needed to imagine what life was like for many in Guatemala in the 1940s, but consider this: from 1949–1951

---

1. Translated and abridged from: Comisión para el Esclarecimiento Histórico, *Memoria del silencio*, chapter 1, volume 1, "Causas y Origenes del Enfrentamiento Armado," available online at shr.aaas.org.

the life expectancy of the indigenous population was thirty-nine years.

Recent history alone cannot explain the armed confrontation . . . In the absence of institutional mechanisms capable of channeling the concerns, demands, and proposals of different groups, a political culture [following independence from Spain in 1821] where intolerance defined the totality of social interaction . . . and voided the possibility of change . . .

If the most visible actors of the conflict were the military and the insurgency, the historical investigation conducted by the CEH provides evidence of the responsibility and participation, in different forms, of segments of the economic elite, political parties, and diverse sectors of civil society. This process involved the entire state, with all of its mechanisms and agents. In this sense, any reduction [of the conflict] to the logic of two actors is not only insufficient, but misleading; a bipolar depiction of the armed conflict does not take into account the actions of political agents, economic forces, or churches. Nor does it explain the constant mobilization and widespread participation of social actors seeking social, economic and political recognition . . . It is impossible to ignore the significance of ideological factors throughout Guatemalan history that contributed to the legitimating framework for violence: the discourse of "official history," the persistence of a racist culture; the doctrine of the armed forces (national honor, authority, and hierarchy) and recent efforts to promote "*ladinización*" [that is, efforts to transform Mayans into ladinos] . . .

The point of this chapter is to understand how Guatemalans constructed their own history; this is the only way to explain the origins and cause of the long armed conflict. It seeks to demonstrate that the war was deeply historically and structurally determined, rooted in the exclusionary, racist, authoritarian and centralist economy, society, and state that took shape in the last century. The landed class, especially that associated with the cultivation of coffee, imposed its economic interests on the state and society . . .

An analysis of the causes of the most tragic period of Guatemalan history requires an understanding of how human relationships and social practices translated into structural, political and social violence . . . Guatemala's 1821 independence did little to alter its entrenched colonial heritage and hierarchical system of social, cultural, and economic relations. During the early years of the republic, the state evolved into an "exclusionary" and racist entity . . . violence in the country has been wielded primarily by the state against the poor and excluded indigenous population . . .

It is difficult to separate structural and political violence. During the period of armed conflict, the state's ever-expanding category of "internal enemy" justified the arbitrary suppression of citizens and democratic rights. Moreover, the National Security Doctrine became the *raison d'être* for army and government policy . . .

Land tenure and economic exclusion

Poverty has been a constant throughout Guatemalan history . . . The social stratification and exclusion that resulted from the inequities of land tenure led to a system of governance characterized by the ongoing use of force to maintain domination. Beginning with the expansion of coffee production in the nineteenth century, the state evolved as the guarantor of the control and supply of labor for vast plantations, thereby contributing to the militarization of national life. The following figures demonstrate recent expressions of this historic form of exclusion: according to the agricultural census of 1950, the first credible source of its kind, 516 large estate owners (*latifundios*) controlled more that 40 percent of land. Meanwhile, 88 percent of small agricultural plots (less than 7 hectares) barely covered 14 percent of farmable lands.

The lack of state-sponsored social policies accentuated this exclusivist dynamic. From 1960 to 1980, Guatemala's longest period of sustained economic growth, state social spending and taxation were the lowest in Central America. Over the course of its existence, the Guatemalan state repeatedly relinquished its role as mediator between divergent social and economic interests. The absence of state mediation facilitated direct conflicts between defenders of the established order (often the prime recipients of state benefits) and citizens forced to fight for their rights.

Within this context, guerrilla movements defended Guatemala's excluded populations, promoting their revolutionary discourse on behalf of the nation's poor.

Racism

Racism, the ideological expression of colonization and subordination, originated during the Spanish invasion.[2] Spanish conquerors relied on racist precepts to justify the oppression and exploitation of the Maya. As they stripped Maya communities of their political and territorial possessions, Spaniards described their actions as a "redemptive and civilizing" enterprise. The Spanish arrival profoundly marked Guatemalan history. Spaniards may have been the first to consider themselves biologically and cultural superior to Indians, yet that belief was later taken up by creoles and finally embraced by ladinos.

---

2. The Spanish conquest of Guatemala began in 1524. This and all subsequent footnotes, along with text in brackets, are the editor's comments. For the CEH's citations, see the original document at shr.aas.org.

The recent history of Guatemala confirms how modes of exclusion and subordination originating with the Spanish invasion persist even today: colonial government, followed by the republican state—controlled by creoles and later ladino elites—ensured that the Maya always occupied the lowest rung of Guatemalan society.

The ideology of "Indian inferiority" evolved from Aristotelian theories of natural inequality, which justified a posteriori an exploitative regime against the indigenous peoples ... The Maya, it was believed, could not reason or govern themselves; they were not subject to natural law ...

As colonial power took shape, indigenous communities responded with legal, violent or passive forms of resistance. They took advantage of colonial law to contest the abuses of colonizers and authorities ... Other forms of resistance against the colonial order incorporated violence, as in the case of local riots or rebellions with broad geographic and temporal reach. Often, uprisings were geared toward the replacement of colonial authorities with indigenous leaders.

After independence, liberalism, enshrined in a new constitution, established equality before the law, and the word "Indian" was eliminated from the texts. This had the effect of eradicating the juridical protection of indigenous social rights that existed under Spanish colonialism, including their inalienable right to communal lands. Independence facilitated the expansion of the large estates, devastating Indian communities ... The independent state attempted to consolidate a national culture based on positivist principles of material development and scientific progress ... "Obligatory and free education for all" was instituted as the main mechanism to achieve this goal. In reality, however, it was nothing more than a formal declaration, and served to reinforce ladino dominance.

The liberal state was characterized by its contradictions.

Policies espoused by government officials may have contained inclusive elements designed to assimilate indigenous groups within a unified culture, yet laws designed to maintain Indians as a distinct group prevailed. The constitution formally declared Indians equal before the law, but other articles in the charter curtailed their rights and imposed obligations from which non-indigenous citizens were exempt. Indians were used as seasonal laborers for coffee plantations and the construction of the nation's infrastructure. A public decree required Indians to work 100–150 days per year on plantations under the control of departmental political bosses. In addition, vagrancy laws imposed fines and sanctions against rural workers who fled plantations, forcing them to work on roads and other public works projects.[3]

The 1945 Constitution, established as part of the October 1944 Revolution, abolished forced Indian labor and similar laws. For the first time in the nation's history, a Constitution recognized the specific rights of indigenous groups and communities, including their inalienable right to communal lands ... The revolution sparked new demands for change; in 1954 the military takeover halted the process [and] initiated the return of forced Indian labor and the dispossession of indigenous lands back into the hands of large ladino landowners ... Based on testimonies recorded by the CEH, forced indigenous labor continued throughout the 1960s ...

Patterns of violence within a society tent to generalize. They are copied and imitated and defuse throughout the social body

---

3. For more on how the liberal Guatemalan state reconciled the rhetorical promotion of equality while politically and legally maintaining and enforcing a biracial apartheid state, see Arturo Taracena Arriola (with Gisela Gellert, et al.), *Etnicidad, estado y nación en Guatemala, 1808–1944* (Antigua, Guatemala, 2002).

and are reproduced across generations. Racism, conscious or unconscious, is an important factor in the explanation of many of the excessive acts of violence committed during the history of Guatemala and the armed conflict. For a racist mentality, any form of indigenous mobilization brings to mind an atavistic uprising. In this way, it can be considered that racism was present in the most bloody moments of the armed conflict, when the indigenous population was punished as an enemy that needed to be vanquished. Poor ladinos were also treated as second-class citizens. Poor and indigenous Guatemalans were marginalized by an exclusionary social model; in turn, political violence tended to feed on itself, reinforcing the model.

Dictatorship and authoritarianism

... Though every one of Guatemala's many constitutions formally established republican governments, complete with a democratic system of elections and separation of powers, dictatorships and military juntas have marked the nation's history. Guatemala has one of the highest rates of military dictatorships in Latin America. This left a deep imprint on the nation's political culture, restricting political expression and citizen participation. Dictatorial governments wielded indiscriminate and unrestrained violence, acting on behalf of elite minority interests ... Over time, an alliance evolved between the government bureaucracy and estate owners, in which the state acted to guarantee the compliance of rural masses. To cite just one example, the 1936 Penal Code, which granted large estate owners police powers, remained in effect until 1973 ... After 1954, a systematic blockade against political participation intensified in the midst of growing fears of communism and the threat of armed struggle. These anxieties justified the worst forms of repression and state terrorism. New authoritarian methods emerged based on unlimited violence. In the name of anti-communism, human rights were systematically, massively, and extensively violated . . .

The 1944 revolution

Guatemala's long authoritarian tradition was interrupted in 1944, when widespread and peaceful protests led to the collapse of General Jorge Ubico's regime. Known as the last "liberal" dictator, Ubico had been in power since 1933. Ubico's downfall ushered in an intense decade of reforms (1944–1954) that created new opportunities for social development and political participation. In 1945, a new constitution expanded the political party system and established a new electoral law. Public education was expanded, especially in the country's interior . . . The Guatemalan Institute of Social Security was created, along with a new Labor Code. At the same time, a land reform promoted the modernization and diversification of the agricultural sector . . . The reforms, government officials argued, were also meant to stimulate industrial development and increase the number of salaried urban workers.

The quick establishment of free elections, proportional representation, and university self-government[4] was a transformational experience for an entire generation of Guatemalans. The 1944 Revolution marked the beginning of a true renovation of social, political and cultural life, a repudiation of the legacies of the liberal past. The creation of the communist Guatemalan Workers Party (PGT) in 1949 and its legalization also broadened the political spectrum.[5]

---

4. The public San Carlos University was granted political autonomy during the October Revolution.

5. For the history of the PGT, Guatemala's communist party, see Gleijeses, *Shattered Hope,* and Grandin, *Last Colonial Massacre.*

The governments of Juan José Arévalo (1944–1951) and Jacobo Arbenz (1951–1954) attempted an ambitious series of reforms in the midst of increasingly charged Cold War antagonisms. The agrarian reform was the most prominent and wide-ranging program, leading to the intensification of domestic ideological and political battles ... Many of the transformations promoted by the 1944 Revolution did not have enough time to produce lasting effects, especially in the judicial realm. The swift incorporation of new rights and the creation of a legitimate parliament ... strained Guatemala's archaic legal system, which remained trapped by colonial structures ... The Labor Code represented a real achievement, however legal structures proved incapable of adjusting to the pace of change. This became even more evident in light of the conflicts generated by the agrarian reform, which threatened entrenched economic, social and political interests.

The agrarian reform

The agrarian reform attempted to restructure Guatemala's land tenure system, long considered the root of oligarchic power and the principal cause of repeated dictatorships and national underdevelopment. In a 1953 speech before congress, President Jacobo Arbenz Guzmán described the Agrarian Reform Law as heralding the beginning of Guatemala's economic transformation. "The law," he said, "is the most precious fruit of the Revolution and the foundation for a new country." The Agrarian Reform promoted agricultural modernization and eliminated feudal labor practices in the countryside. As the text of the law put it ... "all forms of servitude and slavery are hereby abolished, including the use of unpaid and borrowed peasant, migrant, and tenant farm labor ... and the division of indigenous lands. These are prohibited from this time forward, in whatever form they may take."

By 1954, more than 138,000 peasant families had benefitted from the agrarian reforms, the majority of whom were indigenous. This figure translates into an estimated half million people out of a nation of three million. In addition, more than half of the beneficiaries obtained agricultural credits, another factor contributing to the positive reception and impact of agrarian reforms among peasants.

The reforms represented a fierce challenge to the traditional structures of rural power ... Despite the fact that the Agrarian Reform Law was designed to transfer only the unused lands of the largest estates, many communities viewed the law as an opportunity to revive historic communal land conflicts. To cite one example, local indigenous groups from the Cantel municipality in the department of Quetzaltenango, solicited the return of lands granted to ladinos in 1877 by President Justo Rufino Barrios. In 1953, the Departmental Agrarian Commission ruled in favor of the local Indian community.[6]

Despite this triumph, the existing problems of the legal system proved incapable of enforcing the Agrarian Reform Law and resolving the disputes it generated. The inefficiencies of the legal system fueled even more tensions between reform supporters and the communities where the law was enforced; conflicts in the countryside increased the fears of mid-level urban and rural sectors. Threatened by the loss of their strategic interests, many began to back movements that associated the Arévalo and Arbenz governments with communism.

---

6. For more on this conflict in Cantel, see Greg Grandin, "The Strange Case of 'La Mancha Negra': Maya-State Relations in Nineteenth-Century Guatemala," *Hispanic American Historical Review* 77 no. 2 (1997), 211–4.

*The anti-communist campaign and the
overthrow of Jacobo Arbenz*

Anti-communism may have originated outside of Guatemala, yet it assumed its own particular characteristics within the country. In response to the 1932 communist-led peasant insurrection in El Salvador, General Ubico's regime cracked down on weak Marxist and anarchist groups. Despite the fact that movement leaders were sent to prison for thirteen years, Marxist currents gained in strength, especially during ten years of revolutionary governments (1944–1954). Domestic opponents and US officials characterized the reforms of Arévalo and Arbenz—from literary programs to union organizing and strikes—as Soviet-inspired. And by the late forties, anti-communism was no longer just an ideology to confront the government; it was also mobilizing force for political opponents to combat any type of change promoted from above. Members of the military, politicians, the Catholic Church, the media and numerous civil organizations relied on anti-communist beliefs and methods to disrupt the constitutional order. In addition, the legalization of the communist party, the PGT, along with Arbenz's personal friendship with many of its leaders and the participation of its members in the government, fueled the attacks of the right and the Catholic Church ... The Catholic Church assumed a leading role in driving ideological and political polarization ...

Numerous authors have described the role of the United States in the process to foment political instability in Guatemala.[7] At the beginning of 1953, US experts devised a plan to overthrow Arbenz.

---

7. For the 1954 CIA-organized coup, see Nicholas Cullather. *Secret History: The CIA's Classified Account of Its Operations in* Guatemala 1952–54 (Stanford: Stanford University Press, 1999) and Piero Gleijeses, *Shattered Hope: The Guatemalan Revolution and The United States, 1944–1954* (Princeton, 1991).

Following the long years of the Ubico dictatorship, a decade's worth of democratic life awakened the energies and hopes of broad sectors of Guatemalan society. The revolution's mobilizing effect was perhaps even more decisive [in prompting the efforts to] overthrow Arbenz than the material achievements of the brief period of institutional reform. The Constitution of 1945 attempted to reverse the backwardness that penetrated all levels of Guatemalan society. This occurred at the very moment when the world was embarking on a new era following the triumph over fascism and the advancement of capitalist economic development.

For subsequent generations of Guatemalans, the defeat of their modernizing project by the second half of the twentieth century led to deep frustration. The "trauma of '54", as Arbenz's overthrow became known, referred to a mass, collective political effect that ruptured the history of Guatemala and divided its citizens. So drastic was the closing of channels of participation and so extensive was the recourse to violence that it is considered one of the factors that led to the guerrilla insurgency of 1960.

The institutionalization of anti-communism

... Following the fall of Arbenz, anti-communism penetrated the country's collective consciousness. Elite sectors sought revenge and persecuted supporters of the deposed government. As of today, no reliable data exists in terms of repression in the wake of the 1954 coup, though the figures were considerable. Some analysts estimate between 9,000–14,000 arrests, and 2,000–5,000 executions ... On July 19, 1954, the Carlos Castillo Armas[8] regime established the

---

8. Having participated in an earlier failed coup against Arbenz's predecessor, Arévalo, Colonel Castillo Armas fled to Honduras, where he began to work closely with CIA agents to plan the putsch against Arbenz.

National Committee of Defense Against Communism to complete the purge and subordination of internal enemies. The Committee was granted broad powers to organize security forces, investigate cases, and coordinate arrests. The Preventive Penal Law Against Communism also authorized the creation of a register "technically organized, of all persons who have participated in communist activities of any type." The death penalty was later established for individuals who had committed "communist acts of resistance." According to national media sources, between July–November 1954, 72,000 names were added to the communist register . . . The main feature of the Castillo Armas dictatorship was not necessarily the death of political opponents, rather the creation of a generalized atmosphere of insecurity and fear: fear of denunciation, job loss, exile, and political participation. In short, fear justified the existence of a permanent state of exception.

On July 19, 1954, the state took back reallocated lands, and on July 26, it overturned the Agrarian Reform Law. Massive evictions and the persecution of agrarianists (peasants who organized around recuperated lands) followed. Agrarianism became synonymous with "communism," and a beneficiary of the land reforms was considered guilty:

> . . . My father and I had just planted, and that's when things started to get a little ugly . . . they said Arbenz wasn't going to last, and sure enough, the milpa [corn] was ready to harvest when he fell. The people who were with the boss accused us of being communists . . . so I had to flee.
>
> (From testimony taken by the CEH)

> . . . On the Caobanal plantation in 1954, right when Castillo Armas came in . . . everyone who supported Arbenz had to leave

immediately, because they set our houses on fire, with all of the animals still inside . . . my family was lucky to survive.

(From testimony taken by the CEH)

. . . When Jacobo died,[9] they came to get us. The mayor called us and told us to stop the work we were doing and to obey them. Our work on the committees ended right there, and our work on the plantations began.

(From testimony taken by the CEH)

In the regions that experienced the most intense agrarian struggle during the Agrarian Reform and its revocation, CEH witnesses repeatedly referenced the Arbenz era as an important precursor to their later work in peasant leagues, improvement committees, and cooperatives, among many others. Land disputes from the Arbenz period continued up until the most critical years of armed conflict.

. . .

Following the Cuban Revolution, Guatemala, as in the rest of Central America and the Caribbean, became a strategic geopolitical enclave for the United States . . . By identifying all opponents as adversaries, anti-communist governments broadened the scope of the counterinsurgency and expanded persecution methods. In response, civilians were forced to choose between adherence to a repressive regime or silence in order to guarantee precarious survival within a growing atmosphere of state terror . . . By the early 1960s,

---

9. Though it is common for peasant survivors of the 1954 coup to refer to it as "when Jacobo died," Arbenz in fact survived his overthrow, living out the rest of his life in exile in Mexico, Czechoslovakia, and Cuba, among other places. He died in 1971.

instability increased to dangerous levels of permanent ungovernability.[10]

. . .

Citizens, facing constricted margins for social and political organizing, sought out new forms of association. Along the southern coast, and throughout the departments of Chimaltenango and Quiché, *campesinos* organized peasant leagues. In regions that contained large plantations, these leagues focused on workers' rights and legal proceedings to resolve land disputes. In other areas, they organized around public works projects such as bridge construction, roads, schools, and clean drinking water. Peasant mobilization also emphasized the end of forced labor in municipalities and the mismanagement of public funds. The local demands of peasant leagues were linked to larger national issues. New forms of association enabled the exchange of experiences beyond provincial disputes, stimulating the growth of what would later become a robust peasant movement. These leagues were

---

10. Here and at other points in the text, the CEH describes in some detail the complex early-1960s origins of Guatemala's civil war, which include a large military rebellion led by young, reformist military officers, in November 1960, followed by its suppression; massive urban protests led by students and workers in 1962; the formation, led by survivors from the 1960 military rebellion, of Guatemala's first Cold War armed insurgency, the Fuerzas Armadas Rebeldes, associated with a regrouped and now clandestine PGT and allied with Cuba; another US-supported coup, in 1963, aimed at prevented Arevalo from returning to the country to run for president; and, in 1968, the military's first scorched-earth pacification campaign, which killed approximately 8,000 Guatemalans to defeat a few hundred FAR insurgents.

under constant surveillance, subject to assault and systematic persecution by the repressive state apparatus ... The Revolutionary Party (PR, in Spanish), the only quasi-reformist party allowed to operate, organized in rural areas, bringing together members from the ranks of the old revolutionary parties [from the Arévalo and Arbenz governments] ...

Social mobilization during the 1960s was marked by a renovating impulse and by a surge in middle and upper-middle class Catholic student activism. Schools such as the Jesuit-run Liceo Javier, the Maryknoll Sisters Monte María High School, and the Colegio Belga of the Sacred Family[11] participated widely. Crater,[12] the organizational center of the Christian student movement, sent youth volunteers to the countryside during vacation to work in education and health projects. For many who had never seen the misery in which the majority of the population lived, the experience was transformative. For others, student activism had a radicalizing effect, leading to later involvement with the guerrilla movement ...

On May 9, 1967, Guatemalan bishops issued a statement voicing concerns regarding the wave of terror engulfing the nation. "Every day the number of widows and orphans grows," the Bishops said; "Men have been violently ripped from their homes by masked kidnappers. They have been detained in unknown locations and violently assassinated only to appear later as horribly mangled and desecrated corpses. We grieve for our noble and peaceful people, who are living in a state of anxiety, fear and anguish. The insecurity deepens ever more."

---

11. Colegio Belga is the school Rigoberta Menchú attended in the 1970s.

12. Crater was a Maryknoll-run youth organization that became an important center of consciousness raising.

The CEH documented repression in the countryside. Several witness accounts confirm that throughout the 1960s, National Liberation Movement (MLN)[13] militants relied on their relationship with the army to establish political control in rural departments and to restrict the influence of the PR and guerrillas. One CEH key witness recalled the party's influence in Zacapa: *"The MLN party had a grip on everyone. You had to carry a membership card . . . because anyone who had MLN credentials didn't have any problems; it was more valid than your identity card."* . . . In the village of Cajón del Río in the department of Chiquimula, one witness spoke about PR members who fell victim to the MLN: *"The violence began in 1967. Thirteen innocent people accused of being guerrillas died in Cajón de Río. The military commissioners did it. They were pro-liberationists* [MLN party supporters] *and we were not. They were out for retribution. It was the glory days for them, they had all the power."* Landowners with MLN ties also relied on the ideology of anti-communism to violently repress indigenous social demands. In the case of San Vicente Pacaya in the department of Escuintla, old land struggles intensified as a result of the MLN-state alliance.

As social mobilization expanded throughout the countryside, US military assistance also increased. US support spanned the range of Guatemalan military operations and security forces, leading to an escalation of human rights abuses

---

13. Describing itself as the "party of organized violence," the MLN was a quasi-fascist organization that formed following the overthrow of Arbenz, and can best be thought of as the primary agent of death-squad repression in the 1960s and 1970s, both in the countryside and city.

as part of the counterinsurgent war. In an attempt to prevent the rise of guerrilla movements throughout the continent, US governments supplied advisors, training, war materials (vehicles, patrol boats, planes and helicopters), communication devices, technical reinforcements, and logistical assistance for field operations.

The army's counterinsurgent strategy also used civilians to carry out military and intelligence operations and, more importantly, to control the population. Civilians became informants, helped persecute and capture opponents, and carried out acts of repression and terror (torture, disappearances, extrajudicial executions). The involvement of civilian paramilitary forces began in 1966 with the emergence of the so-called "death squads." Of the 35 paramilitary death squads on record, 15 began operations in 1966. Paramilitary members throughout the 1960s were often military commissioners, employees of some of the largest estates, and ultra-right party activists and army supporters.

Statistics documenting the political repression that took place between 1966 and 1970 vary. In November 1968, the Mexican-based Guatemalan Committee for the Defense of Human Rights published a list of 550 cases, both individual and collective, of people assassinated or disappeared between July 1966 and October 1968 . . . According to newspaper accounts, approximately 7,200 Guatemalans were killed or disappeared in the early 1970s. Guerrilla operations were minimal and isolated during this period, yet violence against rural grassroots movements remained steady . . .

In the midst of abiding terror, one horrific event stood out. In May 1978, soldiers from a military detachment in Panzós, Alta Verapaz, violently suppressed a demonstration of peasants demanding lands and protesting against the abuses of large estate owners and local authorities.[14] During the incident, the army massacred 53 q'eqchi peasants and wounded 47 more . . . New rural organizations emerged in the wake of the Panzós massacre. Some evolved along the lines of peasant leagues and cooperatives . . . One CEH witness summarized the dire poverty and frustration experienced by peasants during the period: *"Any past hopes for development were coming to a close. Peasants had spent the last five or six years taking out loans, having a few good years of harvest, but getting deeper into debt in the process . . . Later, with the drop in prices, they were unable to pay back their loans and found themselves in debt to BANDESA [an agricultural bank] . . ."*

As grassroots organizing expanded in the countryside throughout the 1970s, the number of urban protests and demonstrations for better wages also intensified. In 1970, doctors and administrative workers from the Guatemalan Institute of Social Security (IGSS) went on strike. Then on January 20, 1971, the army assassinated Tereso de Jesús Oliva, secretary general of the Independent Peasant Movement . . . Several new unions were founded during the first part of the decade. As union activity increased, so did the repression against it: In June 1972, workers from the Capital Alliance bus company successfully went on strike, however, two months later, their leader, Vicente Mérida Mendoza, disappeared. After a failed 77-day long strike by workers from Atlantic

---

14. For mention of this massacre in *I, Rigoberta Menchú* (London 2009, see page 160; for the decades-long history of PGT organizing that led up to it, see Grandin, *Last Colonial Massacre*; and for its importance in the Mayan cultural and political rights movement, see Betsy Konefal, *For Every Indio Who Falls: A History of Maya Activism in Guatemala, 1960–1990* (Albuquerque, 1990).

Industrial Company, S.A., César Enrique Morataya, the union's secretary general, died in a freak car accident.

On February 4, 1976, an earthquake killed close to 27,000 people, leaving 77,000 wounded and another one million homeless. The disaster exacerbated the already disastrous living conditions of the poor. Widespread human and material losses served as a convenient pretext for companies and businesses to carry out massive layoffs and to violate labor legislation. The earthquake also exposed the weakness of the state, which was adept at counterinsurgent warfare yet totally unequipped to assist the affected population . . . In 1976, more urban and rural strikes occurred than at any other time in Guatemalan history. The upsurge in labor activity triggered a government crackdown in collusion with management sectors. A pastoral letter from the Episcopal Conference of Guatemala released after the earthquake summarized the situation this way, "Guatemala is living in a state of institutionalized violence. In other words, there are unjust social structures and oppression is evident."

Between February 1976 and November 1977, the army repressed peasant movements throughout the department of Quiché, killing 68 cooperative leaders in Ixcán, 40 in Chajul, 28 in Cotzal and 32 in Nebaj. Following the earthquake, the most important labor mobilization was the Pantaleón mill workers strike. The Ixtahuacán Miners March, in November 1977, illustrated the growing alliances between the city and countryside.[15] Following management's announcement of the mine's closure, miners mobilized with the help of the National Workers Union (CNT), and on November 11, 1977, began their march [from the highland department of

---

15. For this strike in *I, Rigoberta Menchú*, p. 161.

Huehuetenango] to the capital. As about 70 miners passed by the communities located along the Pan-American Highway, the workers received widespread political and material support. Upon their arrival at the capital, the marchers were joined by striking Pantaleón mill workers. Press accounts at the time estimated the march to be 150,000 strong by the time it arrived in Guatemala City, its numbers swelled by trade unionists, students, and residents of urban slums. The protest was a milestone that facilitated an alliance between peasants and workers. This became more evident during the Labor Day celebrations of May 1, 1978, which brought together thousands of peasants and trade unionists. It also marked the public debut of the Comité de Unidad Campesina, the CUC.[16]

The indigenous rights movement

The rural movements that emerged in the 1970s were mainly composed of Mayans. Throughout the decade, indigenous participation was distinguished by its size and by the gradual inclusion of new issues alongside traditional peasant claims concerning land, markets, wages, and agricultural prices . . .

Revitalized indigenous organization during the decade was not accidental or short-lived. New leaders evolved over the course of a decades-long process of change from within Mayan communities. Teachers, social workers, technicians, professionals, intellectuals, activists and political leaders took the reigns at community, regional and national levels. Their initiatives contributed to a positive appreciation of Mayan culture, strengthening a sense of "Indian pride," a return to

---

16. Much of Rigoberta Menchú's description of her family's political activity takes place through the CUC. Her father, Vicente, was one of the organization's local founders.

roots, and the defense of indigenous interests. Throughout the 1970s, activists raised awareness of indigenous identity based on its own unique characteristics, not just its difference with non-indigenous Westerners and ladinos.

In order to understand these changes in indigenous communities, along with more radical insurgent tactics, it is important to keep in mind the types of resistance employed by the Maya from the colonial period up through the first half of the twentieth century . . .

The rural movements of the 1970s continued historic forms of resistance, yet they also entailed innovation. Whereas colonial forms of resistance were grounded in local and isolated events, collective action during the seventies encompassed broader and more unified demands. The indigenous movement brought together villages, municipalities and departments from around the country, including a range of linguistic identities that were able to transcend the limited horizons of previous protest. In addition, these new forms of collective mobilization tended to direct their demands at the state, in contrast to past eras when local landowners and politicians mediated larger state interests.

The emergence of the Maya as national social actors was the result of a process of long-term change . . . During the 1940s, evolving religious beliefs sparked tensions within indigenous communities between traditionalists [who defended a syncretistic blend of Mayan and Catholic beliefs and rituals], members of religious brotherhoods, new Catholics and Protestants. At first, religious missionaries focused on combating what they termed the *costumbrismo* of what they considered indigenous paganism. This campaign was especially disrespectful in Quiché (where today the Catholic Church has acknowledged its past ignorance of Mayan culture and tradition). The CEH took testimony from several founders of Catholic Action[17] in Altiplano for whom the acceptance of Catholic rituals provoked great internal contradictions. According to one:

> My father took me with him when my mother sent him to throw the Tzite grains [red seeds used by Mayan priests during religious ceremonies] into the river. He did it in silence and he looked so sad . . . I was eleven then, I'm 51 now, and I couldn't ask him then why he was so sad . . . but on the way back he told me that they were also going to take all of our nahuales [a reference to the sacred Mayan calendar], that it was an order from the priest in Santa Cruz. When we got home, my mother was happy. She was more open to learn how to pray in Spanish, and she understood a lot.

Religious conversion upset the relative power of traditionalists within communities and established regional and national level alliances, such as those among evangelicals and wage-earning ladinos. In some cases, the emergence of wealthy individuals within communities was directly connected to proselytizing and changing beliefs . . . By the late 1940s political parties also began to take interest in municipalities with a majority Maya population. In 1948 alone, 22 Mayan mayors were elected throughout the country. The Catholic Church, along with the Christian Democrats, established social development programs in many rural areas with strong indigenous presence and they helped found cooperatives, improvement

---

17. A catechist movement originally designed to instill orthodox Catholicism and serve as a bulwark against rural communism, Acción Católica evolved in the 1960s and 1970s to be a locus of much of the work associated with liberation theology. Rigoberta Menchú's account of her father, Vicente, focuses on his experience as a catechist in the movement.

committees and peasant leagues. Catholic Action and [the Jesuit-run] Rafael Landívar University supported the education of Mayan youth and fostered leadership training. As part of its mission, Catholic Action worked to create new men and women among its ranks—individuals with the capacity to read and reflect on their social reality based on Christian principles, endowed with the skills to carry out development projects yet aware of the potential risks of developmentalism.

Many of the Mayan youth who returned to their communities from work with Catholic Action learned first hand the extent of ethnic discrimination: despite their training and studies, they lacked the same employment opportunities enjoyed by ladino counterparts. One witness told the CEH that in 1960

> *Catholic Action was very popular in Santa Cruz. I came all the way from the mountains of Zacualpa to Santa Cruz to have a look . . . they talked with us about injustice, they taught us the catechism, the songs and the prayers. Almost all of us were Maya except for two ladinos. We knew about poverty, we Maya have suffered it always. Little by little the people from Catholic Action talked to us about the community of injustices, and little by little we started waking up, we began to understand the way things are.*

. . . Economic transformations [in the early twentieth century] opened indigenous communities and sparked greater interest in events occurring beyond the borders of Indian villages. The improved economic conditions of many indigenous families also coincided with the social reforms of the 1950s, which facilitated educational opportunities in the country's interior. At the same time, however, population growth strained the already stringent land tenure system, contributing to the impoverishment of a large segment of the Mayan peasantry. By the mid 1970s, interest in political participation was on the rise within indigenous communities. The 1974 creation of the Patinamit group, which supported an indigenous candidate's run for congress, led to the formation, in 1976, of the nation's first indigenous party, the National Integration Front. Even though the Front was quickly absorbed into traditional party organizations, it represented a shift in overall Maya political involvement ...

The crisis produced in the wake of the 1976 earthquake led to increased solidarity between communities, especially in the Western Highlands. New relationships among Mayan leaders of various ranks favored an atmosphere of exchange and camaraderie. Within this political climate of dynamic activism, ties between ladino activists, insurgents and Mayan leaders also expanded, especially among those with backgrounds in grassroots organizing.

The CUC was the first nationwide peasant organization distinguished by its Mayan leadership. Several organizations came together to found the CUC, unifying diverse aspirations and demands with a political commitment to social struggle and allowing activists with significant grassroots experience to join forces. As one peasant leader told the CEH:

The seeds of the CUC, the roots of the CUC, came from all over, but it was especially grounded in the Christian commitment ... there were community-based groups that we called 'committed Christians.' In Santa Cruz del Quiché it was Catholic Action ... and there were other groups too, pro-kaqchikel and pro-maya k'iche' groups ... the CUC grew from a series of these small organizations, but let me repeat: they were based on a real Christian commitment. The indigenous focus also began to take shape, though it was more cultural then. But gradually [the CUC] started to call for demands that sparked suspicion for some ladinos. ...

*

. . . By the end of 1978, the number of Mayan mayors in the highlands had increased. Many Mayan political leaders had organizational experience through Catholic Action, cooperatives, peasant leagues, and later, the CUC. Increased indigenous political participation transformed local municipal power structures, which were under the control of the MLN-PID coalition and its regional allies.[18] For its part, the MLN-PID coalition feared the growing alliance between grassroots organizations and Mayan leaders, especially when it raised the possibility of "Indians in power." *"I collaborated with the Christian Democrats, I worked with them on political propaganda to get the votes, so that we could win the municipality,"* one local leader told the CEH. *"We won and from then on they started to check up on us . . . the National Liberation Movement, the MLN, they were all ladinos from the village, and they treated me really bad. They said, 'You're in with the DC* [Christian Democrats], *and you're putting in all those Indian mayors.' That's how they talked to me. It was a real shock for me . . . 'You're putting in all those mayors from the mountains with their ocote torches,'*[19] *they said. And that's how I really got to know what discrimination was."*

State security forces responded to the rise in indigenous political participation with severe repression. Over the course of the 1970s, several indigenous leaders with reformist programs were assassinated, as in the well-known case of José Lino Xoyón, the first indigenous mayor of the departmental capital of Chimaltenango.

---

18. The PID, or Partido Institucional Democrático, was Guatemala's military-run official party in the 1960s and 1970s.

19. *Ocote* is torch pine, associated with nighttime indigenous gatherings.

State violence also led to new associations between Maya leadership and guerrilla movements. These relationships may have demonstrated a shared commitment to justice, yet they did not necessarily result in equal indigenous-ladino alliances. This was due, in large measure, to the predominant "class vision" held by orthodox guerrilla movements at the time. Despite the fact that some guerrilla organizations promoted indigenous claims for social and political recognition, they were not able to formulate proposals to sufficiently express the specific claims of the indigenous as a separate ethnic group, in terms of language, religion, representative authority, and customary law.

The rise of the Guerrilla Army of the Poor

The Guerrilla Army of the Poor (EGP, in Spanish) united members from the Edgar Ibarra Guerrilla Front, Guatemala's first post–Cuban Revolution insurgent group, which conducted training operations in Cuba; the Patriotic Workers' Youth, the Communist Party's youth league, which sent many of it members to study in the German Democratic Republic; and Catholic students from Crater, who worked with peasants in Huehuetenango. The EGP selected the Western Highlands as the starting point for its operations due to the limited army presence in the region. The EGP's strategy divided the country into three zones: mountain, city and plain. The main objective in the mountain region was the formation of a popular guerrilla army, which required the support of poor and mid-level peasants. In the cities, the EGP's social base was the working class. Meanwhile, the agrarian proletariat formed the basis of popular support in the plains, especially along the southern coast. In each zone, the EGP worked to build support among the social base considered an essential force for the revolutionary struggle.

On January 19, 1972, the first EGP column from Mexico entered through Ixcán, north of Quiché. From there, the guerrillas made their way to Huehuetenango and to the southern part of Quiché. Between 1972 and 1978, the EGP focused on establishing a presence in these select areas. On June 7, 1975, the EGP made its public debut when it executed José Luis Arenas, the plantation owner known as the "Tiger of Ixcán." The execution was meant to be symbolic; the army's reaction, however, was swift, sparking the beginning of armed conflict in the region.

Guerrilla-civilian relations and the "indigenous question"

The relationship between guerrilla organizations and the civilian population was complex, for several reasons. These included: fear of admitting collaboration or involvement with the guerrillas; political persecution; the guerrilla practice of "compartmentalizing" information; and the failure of insurgent projects themselves. Experiences varied from community to community, thus caution is necessary regarding any generalizations.

Guerrilla-civilian relations depended, in part, on the specific characteristics of insurgent organizations and the geographic regions in which they operated. According to an EGP document:

> The political struggle of the masses and armed struggle come together in the People's Revolutionary War . . . but not in the same way . . . in the mountains, armed struggle is the fundamental form of mass struggle, and its complement. In contrast, in the capital and in other major cities, mass struggle is the fundamental basis of the fight. Military struggle and mass struggle are united as one only at the end of the war, in insurrections.

EGP support grew from grassroots community organizations in the Western Highlands, the consciousness-raising activities of the Catholic Church, peasant leagues, and the Christian Democratic Party . . . EGP activists began to organize during the 1970s, teaching guerrilla goals, and training local community leaders in self-defense and weapons. As mentioned above, the 1976 earthquake exposed the country's vast social and economic inequalities and the state's inability to manage the relief effort. This led to new ties of solidarity and communication between communities and insurgent organizations. Insurgent groups took advantage of this climate in the wake of the disaster, mixing social demands with the goals of armed struggle. According to one CEH witness: "*Community leaders were promoting revolution to reclaim lands . . . to get a good education, to respect dignity, because back then there was no freedom of speech, no right to organize, etc.*"

In contrast to the EGP, another insurgent organization, the Revolutionary Organization of People in Arms (ORPA, in Spanish), separated clandestine armed operations from social and economic protest. As one ex-ORPA member told the CEH, "*Mixing union, peasant and student movements with the guerrilla struggle was very dangerous. [We believed] it would have only resulted in bloody repression . . . we had to maintain and respect the division between legal battles and clandestine armed movements.*"

In comparison to the heavily Mayan zones where the EGP operated [which experienced hundreds of massacres], ORPA's separation of civilians from the clandestine armed vanguard, in addition to the group's relative lack of political and territorial influence, resulted in a much smaller number of destroyed rural communities during the 1981–1982 army offensive. The fact that the EGP did not maintain a division between legal and armed forms of struggle explains both its influence among guerrilla organizations and the reasons why rural communities within its area of control were so hard hit during the counterinsurgent campaigns. According to one indigenous ex-combatant from Chimaltenango:

> You have to understand the real causes of the war. It's not as if the war came out of nowhere. A guerrilla group would arrive in a village, for example, and they'd say, 'Look, we have to fight for this and this.' The guerrillas didn't invent those things . . . For example, my parents, they were from the generation of 1944 and they knew all about the achievements of the revolution. And so the people got excited.

For one young K'iche' leader and guerrilla fighter, the

> historical memory of poor indigenous people is very potent, but it is strongest when it involves the memory of a historical claim, the memory of political demands, and an awareness that this is not their system, that this is not their state . . . all of that came together . . . the historic possibility for liberation, to change the system. Sure, the guerrillas announced the possibility of overthrowing the Lucas regime[20] and installing a revolutionary government. And this ignited people.

While guerrilla groups attempted to broaden their social base and gain supporters, many Mayan leaders viewed the insurgency as a way to advance their own movements. Other activists who saw their efforts to change through institutional channels frustrated by repression saw the insurgency as an opportunity for radical transformation. As one witness told the CEH:

> I am a poor peasant . . . my mother and my father were true peasants, migrant workers along the coast. I was seven when I started to travel with my father along the coast. We were on the coast for a

---

20. General Romeo Lucas García was president of Guatemala from 1978 to 1982.

long time because we didn't have lands of our own . . . When I was
19, I participated in a wage strike on the Pantaleón de Escuintla
plantation . . . they fired the majority of us, we were mostly cane
workers . . . That was the last time that I worked for the bosses along
the coast . . . I joined the guerrillas on December 12, 1980.

Escalating violence and state militarization (1979–1985)

Violence spiraled to unimaginable levels between 1979 and
1985. The governments of generals Romeo Lucas García and
Efraín Ríos Montt concentrated their efforts on the annihilation of internal enemies. They systematically attacked not
only the guerrillas, but also the grassroots social movements
and civilians located in areas with a strong guerrilla presence
and a majority Maya population . . .

The terror unleashed during the Lucas García government
(1978–1982) destroyed remaining social, political and profes-
sional organizations. The systematic murder and disappearance of well-known leaders, in addition to the massacre of
peasants in the country's interior, provoked strong international repercussions. Due to the intensity of state repression, Guatemala became the target of frequent sanctions and
diplomatic isolation. As the human rights situation dete-
riorated, the US upheld military restrictions passed in 1977
during the Carter administration. However, US military aid
financed through the Military Assistance Program, which
started before the 1977 aid ban was passed, remained in effect.
Commercial sales and foreign military sales [of military
equipment] also continued, as did credits for the purchase of
arms. In 1974, Guatemala signed a military treaty with Israel.
Between 1975 and 1982, the Guatemalan army acquired 11
planes and 10 combat tanks from Israel. They came equipped
with Galil missiles totaling US$6 million. In 1979, the Israeli
government helped build a Guatemalan military factory in

Alta Verapaz to produce ammunition for Galil assault weapons and Uzi machine guns. Israeli technicians from Tadiran Israel Electronics Industries installed a computer center in Guatemala City, which began operating in 1980. The next year, the army inaugurated the School for Broadcasting and Electronics, constructed and equipped with the support of Israeli intelligence specialists . . .

From the late 1970s on, the state intensified a strategy of select repression, targeting movement leaders, such as Mario Mujía Córdoba, the senior advisor to the Ixtahuacán miners, who was assassinated on July 20, 1978 . . . In October 1978, an increase in public transportation fares triggered six weeks of widespread protest. According to one source, the clashes resulted in 40 deaths, 300 wounded, and more that 1,500 arrests. Shortly thereafter, Oliverio Castañeda de León, one of the main protest leaders and secretary general of the University Student Association, was killed after participating in anniversary celebrations to commemorate the October 1944 Revolution. Throughout the decade, social mobilization tended to peak during the funerals of prominent movement leaders. Burials often sparked massive protests, and national and internal condemnation of the military. In their mourning, tens of thousands of protesters would march in silence through the streets holding red carnations in their left hands. Police reprisals, even at funerals, led to more casualties and further exposed the repressive nature of the counterinsurgent state.

The insurgency fortified links with grassroots movements as repression intensified. The EGP influenced organizations such as the CUC, the Robin García Revolutionary Student Front, Revolutionary Christians (CR), among many others. Widespread repression also galvanized efforts to unite organizations, including the National Committee on Trade-Union

Unity (CNUS) in 1976; the 1979 formation, following an upsurge in state violence, of the Democratic Front Against Repression; and the creation, in 1981, of the January 31 Popular Front (FP-31).[21] State violence began to target these organizations. The murder of the social democrat, Alberto Fuentes Mohr, on January 22, 1979, marked the beginning of a wave of political assassinations. As violence against political leaders increased, space for political dialogue collapsed . . . In March 1979, Manuel Colom Argueta, leader of the recently registered United Front of Revolution was murdered during a high-speed car chase in the middle of Guatemala City. Between 1978 and 1981, 19 FUR and 15 Democratic Socialist Party leaders were murdered. Universities also came under fire by the end of the decade. According to the University Student Association, more than 100 USAC students and professors were killed . . .

By the late seventies, violence in the department of Quiché did not discriminate between armed insurgents, members of grassroots movements and the rest of the civilian population. In light of this situation, peasant leaders, including several CUC members, traveled to Guatemala City to denounce the repression before national and international audiences. While in the capital, they met with students, trade unionists, shantytown residents and the press. Following the refusal of newspapers to publish their reports of repression, peasant leaders occupied the Spanish Embassy on January 31, 1980. Despite the Spanish ambassador's attempts to prevent the indiscriminate use of force, the army set fire to the embassy, killing 37 people inside.[22] The ambassador made it out alive, as did one

---

21. The Menchú family was associated with many of these organizations. See *I, Rigoberta Menchú*, 231–33.

22. Including Rigoberta Menchú's father, Vicente. See *I, Rigoberta Menchú*, chapter 15.

peasant, who was kidnapped from the hospital where he was recuperating only to be tortured and later executed . . .

Following the organization of a sugar cane workers strike between February and March 1980, which drew the support of more than 70,000, the CUC became the face of indigenous activism. The strike united for the first time permanent coastal workers with migrant highland workers.[23] The takeover of the Spanish Embassy, together with the cane workers strike—both promoted by CUC activists—represented the high point of political and social activism during the early eighties. The actions demonstrated the convergence of both grassroots social organizations and the insurgency. This became even more evident on May 1, 1980, when the CNUS, which had come to symbolize movement unity, called for the "establishment of a popular, democratic and revolutionary government" to "overthrow the Lucas García" regime. Insurgent groups widely supported the CNUS appeals. Thirty-two demonstrators were kidnapped near the Parque Centenario following the announcement. The tortured remains of 28 appeared a few days later. Shortly after these murders, in June 1980, 27 members of the Central Nacional de Trabajadores were forcefully disappeared. Then in August, 17 trade unionists and university students, all activists with the Union Orientation School, were kidnapped . . .

The guerrilla offensive

The insurgent offensive launched in 1980 is considered the beginning of widespread guerrilla war . . . The incorporation of rural sectors into guerrilla forces produced contradictory effects. Many insurgents maintained an overly confident belief in swift military victory. Often this was due to the demands

---

23. For this strike in *I, Rigoberta Menchú*, see chapter 32.

of individuals eager to enlist, even when guerrilla forces lacked the capacity to absorb new recruits and fit them into a military framework ... The army took advantage of what it considered a guerrilla error in dispersing insurgent forces throughout the country. Accordingly, the military adapted its objectives to "neutralize" civilian support before directly targeting insurgent military units. The army high command understood that guerrilla forces controlled several municipalities throughout the departments of Quiché, Huehuetenango, Chimaltenango, and Sololá, in addition to exerting influence throughout the departments of San Marcos, Baja and Alta Verapaz, Totonicapán and Quetzaltenango. Military officials calculated that close to 270,000 civilians were organized by the guerrillas in differing degrees of involvement. In addition to these considerations, they also believed that the department of Chimaltenango ... was an imminent threat to the [nearby] capital of Guatemala City; [the military feared] that Chimaltenango was positioned to be declared liberated territory, given the region's massive insurgent support, an action that would invite even more international scrutiny.

Scorched earth

On March 23, 1982, a group of young army officers seized power through a military coup. They vowed to continue the counterinsurgent struggle and to improve the technical and operational capacity of the military ...

The Catholic Church and social organizations rejected the evangelical fundamentalism of the coup-installed president, General Efraín Ríos Montt.[24] Ríos Montt was a member of

---

24. For Ríos Montt, see Virginia Garrard-Burnett, *Terror in the Land of the Holy Spirit: Guatemala under General Efrain Ríos Montt, 1982–1983* (Oxford, 2010).

the "El Verbo," an evangelical church, which belonged to Gospel Outreach, a California-based Pentecostal group. Upon taking power, Ríos Montt appointed two members of his church as secretary of private affairs and as his personal presidential secretary. During his weekly television and radio programs, Ríos Montt addressed the nation with moralizing messages about personal conduct, family life, and civic responsibility. Protestant churches located in conflict zones received preferential treatment over the course of Ríos Montt's presidency (1982–1983). In comparison to the social ministry of the Catholic Church, the seemingly apolitical and "passive" gospel preached by evangelical churches was incorporated into the counterinsurgent strategy to control rural communities. The anti-communism, spiritualism, and submission to authority promoted by evangelical ministries found fertile ground in the countryside under army control. While Catholics suffered persecution and repression, evangelical churches flourished . . . In many areas, the army intentionally involved evangelicals in counterinsurgent operations. According to one evangelical witness: *"Some [evangelicals] participated openly in the civil patrols. There were even a lot of pastors who were also patrol leaders, or military commissioners, or spies . . . there were some who denounced people to the army, even other evangelicals. They had to name names because they were the army's ears and informants."* In many regions, residents were forced to carry an identity card indicating their religion. One CEH witness recalled: *"If you were evangelical things were calmer. We Catholics always ran greater risk, that's why many people became evangelicals."*

The counterinsurgent strategy implemented during the Lucas García dictatorship expanded during the reign of Ríos Montt. Indeed, military campaigns known as "Ash '81," "Victoria '82," and "Firmness '83" represented the high point of military repression. The army defined its objectives through metaphors such as "to remove the water from the fish," in reference to internal security, or the phrase, "winning the hearts of the population," to refer to socio-economic development . . .

Since 1981, the army had been conducting an internal evaluation, which led to the following conclusion. According to General Héctor Alejandro Gramajo: "The insurgents received support not because of the inherently subversive nature of the civilian population; rather because of deeply rooted and long-term problems that exist within the social system." . . . Within this new framework, the army viewed indigenous participation in grassroots organizing or the insurgency as a result of a lack of integration into the state and a weak sense of nationhood. Fueled by historic racism, the army argued that Indians were fundamentally immature and therefore easily manipulated by guerrilla political activities . . . In a controversial interview from 1982, Francisco Bianchi, Ríos Montt's spokesperson, declared: "The guerrillas conquered many indigenous collaborators, so the indigenous are subversive, right? And how do you fight against the insurgency? Clearly, we'd have to kill the Indians because they were collaborating with the subversion." . . . As Ríos Montt himself indicated: "Naturally, if a subversive operation exists where Indians are involved with guerrillas, then Indians will die. However, it's not the army's philosophy to kill Indians, rather to re-conquer and help them."

Defining the civilian population as a potential threat was the starting point for the annihilation of social organizations, in addition to the massacre and destruction of hundreds of communities across the country. Beginning in 1981, the army attempted to control and neutralize civilians through Civil Defense Patrols (PAC). Civil patrols organized male

community members into local defense units, endowed with
punitive capabilities, and in support of military actions. The
PAC carried out internal surveillance of communities, in addition to participating in military operations, as many reports
have confirmed. The PAC constituted new, militarized local
power structures that further destroyed the social fabric of
rural communities and traditional social relations. In reference to the PAC, a former Guatemalan president told the CEH:

> It was the first time in Guatemalan history that indigenous people
> felt useful. It was the first time in the nation's history that indig-
> enous people felt used, utilized because of necessity by the army,
> government, president and economic sectors. It was the first time
> that indigenous people saw themselves as indispensable to their
> bosses, because they were the ones that could stop the spread of the
> guerrillas, and they did it with a rifle in hand. A patrol member
> once said to me: 'Ah! It's more important to carry a rifle. It doesn't
> matter if it hangs from your right or left shoulder.'

Events in Guatemala [between 1981 and 1983] did not signal the
total destruction of the Guatemalan National Revolutionary
Unity (URNG),[25] however, the group's defeat, which became
evident by 1983, led to a social and military retreat. As the
URNG lost initiative, the army filled the void . . .

Part two: the massacres[26]

The large number of military operations resulting in the
slaughter of defenseless civilians—commonly known as

---

25. Organized in 1982 as the umbrella organization of
Guatemala's main insurgent organizations.

26. Translated and abridged from: Comisión para el
Esclarecimiento Histórico, chapter 2, volume 3, "Violaciones de los
Derechos Humanos," *Memoria del silencio*, "Masacres."

massacres—is one of the most indelible features of the armed conflict in Guatemala. Sixty-four percent of the massacres documented by the CEH occurred between June 1981 and December 1982, in addition to 76 percent of arbitrary executions. This eighteen-month period represented the high point of military violence, the most death, destruction and pain in the nation's contemporary history.

In the majority of cases, massacres were not limited to the mass execution of individuals. They included barbarism that is difficult to believe upon first reading. For the witnesses and victims, however, the images are still fresh in their minds: beheaded corpses; mutilated bodies; pregnant women with their bellies slashed open by machete or bayonet; impalement; "the smell of burnt flesh"; cadavers devoured by dogs. These scenes speak to the reality of what occurred. Such acts were repeated throughout dozens of communities, and recalled by thousands of people who gave their testimony individually or collectively. In addition to other credible sources gathered by the CEH, the truth of the massacres is undeniable. In addition, exhumations of massacre sites have provided material proof of the brutality of how the killings were executed.

Massacres included the widespread plunder of victims' material belongings, and the destruction of homes, crops, animals, pots, grinding stones and clothes. These operations have been described as part of the army's "scorched earth" campaign. For tens of thousands of individuals in the five departments where the massacres were concentrated, life was ripped apart. The physical, but most especially psychic, traces reverberate through communities even today.

From violence to barbarism

... Figures alone do not convey the impact of massacres. That requires a qualitative analysis that captures both [the

importance of massacres in the] tactical and strategic logic of
the military, as well as the horror they produced among the
victims. The February 13, 1982, massacre of civilians in village
of Chisís . . . located in the department of Quiché, is indica-
tive of the scope and scale of the majority of massacres investigated by the CEH.

Chisís is located in Ixil, a region characterized by extreme
poverty, neglect on the part of national institutions, and skewed
concentration of land ownership. Added to these conditions, a
strong culture of racism imbued all socioeconomic relations;
ladinos controlled the large plantations, while the Ixil owned
very small parcels. By the mid 1970s, the EGP began organizing throughout the region, and a few weeks before the Chisís
massacre, insurgents attacked a military detachment in San
Juan Cotzal. Following the attack, on January 19, 1982, soldiers
arrived in Chisís and called a meeting with village leaders.
They came with a list of suspected guerrilla collaborators. Four
men whose names appeared on the list were captured and
later disappeared. That day, the army also forced men from the
community to join the civil patrols. On February 11, 1982, the
guerrillas attacked a helicopter flying close to Chisís. Again, the
response was swift: two days later, on February 13, the army,
accompanied by civil patrols from San Juan Cotzal, occupied
Chisís and massacred close to 200 people. A group of CEH
witnesses and survivors narrated the details of the slaughter:

> The army came into Chisís from Santa Avelina. A few other groups
> came from Tztinay and another from Secal, a village over by that way.
> Three groups . . . at around five in the morning . . . the soldiers entered
> without a sound, they entered our village without any commotion.
>
> Many people went out at dawn to go shopping at the market. When
> they met up with the soldiers, the soldiers said to the men and

women, 'Go back, go back home, there are more of us coming, and we are going to talk.' So little by little, people started going back to their houses . . . The soldiers said 'pleased to meet you,' and the people went back to their houses feeling secure.

Many groups of soldiers occupied our village. They surrounded it and put up fences, and the people felt safe because the soldiers were organizing it all. Nobody was going to leave our houses because we trusted them.

The people were all organized by the soldiers and the civil patrols were already armed. The people trusted the soldiers. And then the soldiers came and said, 'How are you? Good morning, good morning, go inside your houses.'

They didn't round up people. They went house by house, coming little by little, spreading like a fire.

My husband burned to death inside my house. The soldiers and the patrols came to kill my husband. They burned everything in my house, even my grinding stones, my machetes, my clothes, everything.

They raped his wife Juana in front of his niece, then they tied her up in front of all the children . . . later they set the house on fire. When they set the house on fire, everyone was alive and bound together. That's what happened to everyone they found inside their houses. They burned everyone alive.

The soldiers would enter a house and round up the whole family, even little kids like seven years old. They would tie up the men and kill the children while the men were already tied up. They would make them watch as they were burning their children alive, and also their houses.

We were hearing the noises, the screams coming from inside the other houses. We heard them beating people and my uncle said that we should all get out of there. But my grandfather said no. He said, 'If you're scared, leave. I have my authority and I am going to fulfill my duty . . .' My grandfather had a staff from the mayor of San Juan Cotzal that was like a symbol of authority. He said that the army wasn't going to do anything to him because he had power. He showed the soldiers his staff and they threw it on the fire, and then they tied them up inside the house.

A civil patrol was on the town border. They were a group of about 20 young guys hanging a flag when the soldiers approached them . . . the soldiers said, 'What's up? How are you doing?' And they answered, 'We're patrolling.' The soldiers ordered them to stand in a line . . . the twenty of them got into a line and the soldiers blew their heads off, they stabbed them, hacked at them with machetes, and shot them.

Because the civil patrols didn't want to kill their own people, they took ten and shut them inside a house. They massacred them right there at point blank range, all ten at the same time, as if they were killing ants with poison.

Who knows how many members of the army came here to massacre the people, to set our houses on fire, and burn down our homes, our corn, our beans, our blankets . . . We left without clothes . . . everyone, even pregnant women and young children, everyone that was inside their houses, they all died because of the army.

They burned my grandmother alive there. She was nothing more than bones, and the dogs ate her, it must have tasted good because the flesh was burnt, right? . . .

The Chisís massacre illustrates several features of military operations against communities suspected of having guerrilla ties. These include: military tactics such as the element of surprise; the use of deception and the enclosure of the village;

the participation of the PAC and military commissioners to implicate civilians [in the violence]; and the use of terror and extreme cruelty to paralyze the population and to definitively isolate the community from the guerrillas. Following the logic of "draining water from the fish," military operations attempted the physical, cultural and spiritual destruction of communities through the elimination of their human and material means of sustenance. All of these elements figured repeatedly in massacres during the height of armed confrontation.

Part three: conclusions[27]

The Commission for Historical Clarification was established . . . to render an objective, fair and impartial accounting of human rights violations and acts of violence linked to the armed conflict that caused suffering for the people of Guatemala. When the members of the CEH were appointed, we had, to varying degrees and based on our own life experiences, a general understanding of events. Two [of the three] commission members are Guatemalans, however, and we lived the entire tragedy in our native land and, in one way or another, suffered through it. Still, we couldn't have imagined the magnitude—Dantesque in its horror—of what took place.

We received thousands of testimonies. We stood alongside survivors during such emotional moments as when the bodies of loved ones were exhumed from clandestine cemeteries. We interviewed former heads of state, high-ranking members of the military, and guerrilla leaders. We read thousands of pages

---

27. Translated and abridged from: Comisión para el Esclarecimiento Histórico, *Memoria del silencio*, "Conclusiones y Recomendaciones del Informe del CEH."

of documents from a diverse range of civil society organizations. The Commission's report takes all of these versions into account, and brings together what we heard, saw, and read about so many atrocities and brutalities. The truth will benefit us all, both victims and victimizers. This is undeniable. The victims, whose past has been degraded and manipulated, will be dignified. At the same time, perpetrators will be able to recover the dignity that they deprived themselves of through recognition of their immoral and criminal acts.

Thousands are dead. Thousands mourn. For those who remain, reconciliation is impossible without justice. In the words of our Nobel Laureate, Miguel Angel Asturias, "The eyes of the buried will close together on the day of justice, or they will never close."

The tragedy of the armed confrontation

The 1962 outbreak of domestic armed confrontation plunged Guatemala into one of the most tragic and devastating periods of its history, leaving behind enormous human, material, institutional and moral costs. Over the course of its work documenting human rights violations and acts of violence related to the period of armed conflict, the Commission for Historical Clarification registered a total of 42,275 victims, including men, women, and children. Of these, 23,671 were victims of arbitrary execution, and 6,159 were forcefully disappeared. Based on the number of fully identifiable victims, 83 percent were Maya and 17 percent were ladino. When these figures are combined with data from other investigations of political violence in Guatemala, the CEH estimates the total number of dead and disappeared as a result of the fratricidal confrontation at more than 200,000.

The Commission for Historical Clarification has concluded that Guatemalan economic, cultural, and social relations were shaped by profound exclusions, antagonisms, and conflicts reflected in the nation's colonial past. From independence in 1821, an event led by the country's elite, an authoritarian state was created that excluded the majority of Guatemalans; it was racist in theory and practice, and served to protect the interests of a small, privileged elite. Throughout Guatemalan history, particularly during the period of armed conflict, state violence has been fundamentally aimed against the excluded, the poor, and the Maya, as well as those who struggled in favor of a just and more equitable society.

Guatemala's anti-democratic political tradition is based on an economic system characterized by the concentration of material goods and resources in the hands of a small minority. This fundamental inequality formed the basis of a regime of multiple exclusions, bolstered by a culture of racism, which became the most profound expression of violent and dehumanizing social relations. The state emerged gradually as an instrument to safeguard this economic system and to guarantee ongoing exclusion and injustice.

Thus a vicious circle was created in which social injustice led to protest and subsequently to political instability, to which there were always only two responses: repression or military coups.

Confronted by movements calling for economic, political, social, or cultural change, the state increasingly resorted to terror in order to maintain social control. Political violence was thus a direct expression of structural violence ... The need to respond to legitimate claims and social demands led to the Guatemalan state creating an intricate repressive apparatus, which replaced the legal system [that is, responding to conflicts, which in a functioning democracy would have been solved through the courts, with terror]. This illegal, underground punitive system was orchestrated and directed by military intelligence. Over the course of the internal armed confrontation, the state relied on repression as the main form of social control, in direct and indirect collaboration with dominant economic and political sectors.

The 1954 overthrow of Colonel Jacobo Arbenz's government accelerated the breakdown of political freedom and expression. New restrictive legislation, inspired by fundamentalist anti-communism, suppressed a wide-ranging and diverse social movement, placing even further constraints on an already exclusionary political system ... Added to legal restrictions, from 1963 on, increased state repression against real or imagined opponents constituted another decisive factor in the closing off of political options for Guatemala.[28]

The CEH recognizes that the advance of state and society towards polarization, militarization, and civil war was not only an effect of national history. The Cold War also played a critical role. Right-wing political parties and diverse sectors of the Guatemalan elite embraced the anti-communism promoted by the foreign policy of the United States. Meanwhile, US governments were more than willing to lend support to strong military regimes located within their nation's strategic sphere of influence. Anti-communism and the National Security

---

28. Washington supported a second coup in 1963, to prevent the reformist Juan José Arévalo, who was the first president following the 1944 revolution, from running for re-election. The construction of a full counterinsurgent apparatus—including death squads run by a centralized intelligence agency—was put into place following this coup. For the immediate post-1954 counterinsurgency, see Stephen Streeter, *Managing the Counterrevolution: The United States and Guatemala, 1954–1961* (Athens, OH, 2000); for post-1963 repression, see Grandin, *Last Colonial Massacre.*

Doctrine formed part of US anti-Soviet strategy throughout Latin America. In Guatemala, this strategy was first expressed in anti-reformist, then anti-democratic policies, culminating in a criminal counterinsurgency. The National Security Doctrine found fertile ground in Guatemala. Anti-communist thought took hold in the 1930s in defense of religion, and the conservative traditions and values that were allegedly under attack due to the global expansion of atheistic communism. The Catholic Church vociferously supported these ideas up through the 1950s. The church hierarchy labeled "communist" any position that challenged its official discourse, thereby fueling even more division and confusion within Guatemalan society.

The Catholic Church began to abandon its conservative stance in the wake of the Second Vatican Council (1962–1965) and the Episcopal Conference of Medellín (1968), both of which advocated and prioritized work with excluded, poor, and marginalized sectors to promote a more just and equal world. These doctrinal and pastoral changes came into direct conflict with the counterinsurgency, which viewed Catholics as potential guerrilla allies and internal enemies, subject to persecution, death, or exile. For their part, guerrilla movements recognized liberation theology as a way to gain the trust of communities, and to expand social support networks. A large number of catechists, lay activists, nuns, priests, and missionaries fell victim to the violence. Their lives are further testament to the cruelty of the armed conflict.

The Guatemalan insurgency emerged as the response of one sector of the population to the nation's diverse structural problems. In light of endemic injustice, poverty, and discrimination, insurgents called for the construction of a new social, political, and economic order through the forceful takeover of power. Throughout the armed conflict, guerrilla groups adhered to Marxist doctrine in its diverse international forms. Although many insurgent organizations shared a common history in the proscribed communist Guatemalan Workers Party (PGT), several groups came together as a result of their criticism of the PGT's renunciation of armed struggle.

The Cuban Revolution and its support of armed struggled influenced events in Guatemala and the rest of Latin America ... As state repression intensified and as the pool of potential victims grew, the insurgency gained in strength. While guerrilla groups may not have shared a specific ideological-political platform, the insurgents were united by their belief in the primacy of armed struggle as the only national-political solution for Guatemala ... The state relied on the concept of an internal enemy to deliberately exaggerate the military threat of the insurgency. The inclusion of all opponents—whether pacifist or guerrilla, legal or illegal, communist or non-communist—under one label justified multiple and serious criminal acts. In the face of widespread political, social, and cultural opposition, the state resorted to military operations geared towards the physical annihilation or total intimidation of the opposition. Based on the concept of the internal enemy, the CEH has determined why the vast majority of the victims of state violence were unarmed civilians and not guerrilla fighters.

Data analyzed by the CEH also revealed significant differences among victims of state violence based on the geographic concentration of military operations, and the specific period of armed confrontation. From 1962–1970, state military operations focused on the eastern part of the country, Guatemala City, and the southern coast. During this period, violence affected mainly peasants, rural trade unionists, university instructors, teachers, students, and guerrilla sympathizers. From 1971–1977, repression was more selective and geographically dispersed, targeting community activists, union leaders, catechists, and students. Military operations during the most violent and bloody period of armed conflict (1978–1985) were concentrated in the departments of Quiché, Huehuetenango, Chimaltenango, Alta and Baja Verapaz, the southern coast and the capital. The majority of victims were indigenous Maya and, to a lesser extent, ladino. During the final period of armed conflict (1986–1996), repression was more selective, affecting Maya and ladino populations almost equally.

The state was responsible for 93 percent of human rights violations and incidents of violence documented by the CEH.

CEH findings have confirmed that the massacres carried out by state agents between 1981–1983 in Quiché, Huehuetenango, Chimaltenango, Alta Verapaz and Baja Verapaz represented the most heinous of a series of military operations directed against the noncombatant civilian population ... The CEH concluded that operations intended to destroy, in whole or in part, Maya communities in the four above-mentioned regions constituted attempts to inflict "serious bodily or mental harm to members of the group" (Article II.b of the "Convention on the Prevention and Punishment of the Crime of Genocide").[29] The destruction of social cohesion that was often the result of military operations corresponded to an attempt to annihilate groups physically and spiritually. The investigation also proved that the killings, especially indiscriminate massacres, were accompanied by the widespread razing of villages. In

29. For the full discussion of how the CEH made its genocide ruling, see *Memoria del silencio*, volume 2, chapter 3.

the Ixil region, for example, 70–90 percent of villages were destroyed, including the persecution of the indigenous population during displacement.

CEH analysis has uncovered the coordination of national military structures to enable the "effective" action of soldiers and patrols in the execution of army operations. For example, the Victoria Plan '82 stipulated: "the mission is to annihilate the guerrillas and parallel organizations." During the Firmness '83–1 campaign, the army determined that it would carry out its operations "with a maximum of civil patrol (PAC) members, in order to raze all collective works . . ."[30] The intention to destroy, in whole or in part, Mayan communities was not expressed in isolated events or the excesses of undisciplined soldiers. Nor was it the result of independent action on the part of mid-level army officers. With great consternation, the CEH has determined that many of the massacres and human rights violations committed against indigenous groups were part of a higher, strategically planned policy, translated into actions that followed a logical and coherent sequence.

The CEH therefore concludes that agents of the Guatemalan state . . . committed acts of genocide against the Maya people between 1981–1983 . . . This conclusion is based on evidence, considered in light of Article II of the [United Nations] "Convention on the Prevention and Punishment of the Crime of Genocide," that: 1) massacres of Mayan people occurred (Article II.a); 2) serious bodily or mental harm was inflicted (Article II.b); and 3) the group was deliberately

---

30. Since the release of the CEH report, further documentation related to these plans has been made public. See National Security Archive, "Operation Sofia: Documenting Genocide in Guatemala," available online at www.gwu.edu.

subjected to living conditions calculated to bring about its physical destruction in whole or in part (Article II.c). This conclusion is also based on evidence that acts were committed "with intent to destroy, in whole or in part" groups identified by their common ethnicity, by reason thereof, whatever the cause, motive or final objective of these acts may have been (Article II, first paragraph).

Guerrilla violence accounts for 3 percent of the violations registered by the CEH.

Suggestions for Further Reading

Over the last decade, scholars have researched many of the events discussed in Menchú's memoir. For peasant and indigenous mobilization in the 1960s and 1970s, along with the Comité de Unidad Campesina's relationship to the EGP, see Matilde González's two-volume *Se cambió el tiempo—* Vol. 1: *Conflicto y poder en territorio K'iche'*; Vol. 2: *Historias de vida y tradición oral de San Bartolomé Jocotenango, Quiché* (Guatemala City: Asociación para el Avance de las Ciencias Sociales en Guatemala, 2002)—and Carlota McAllister, *The Good Road: Conscience and Consciousness in a Postrevolutionary Mayan Village* (Durham: Duke University Press, forthcoming). For the indigenous rights movement of the 1970s, especially as it related to indigenous beauty pageants, see Betsy Konefal, *For Every Indio Who Falls: A History of Maya Activism in Guatemala, 1960–1990* (Albuquerque: University of New Mexico Press, 2010). For the 1980 southern coast strike, see Elizabeth Oglesby, "Politics at Work: Elites, Labor and Agrarian Modernization in Guatemala 1980–2000," PhD thesis, Department of Geography, University of California, Berkeley, 2002; for a regional study of the insurgency that traces land conflicts back to the overthrow of Arbenz and earlier, see Greg Grandin, *The Last Colonial Massacre: Latin America in the Cold War* (Chicago: University of Chicago Press, 2004), which also describes the 1978 Panzós massacre. For urban violence, see Deborah Levenson, *Trade Unionists against Terror: Guatemala City, 1954–1984* (Chapel Hill: University of North Carolina Press, 1994).

Also consult the UN truth commission report: Comisión para el Esclarecimiento Histórico (Commissión for Historical Clarification, CEH), *Guatemala: Memoria del silencio.* Twelve volumes (Guatemala City: United Nations Operating Projects Services, 1999). The CEH report, in Spanish, and an English-language summary of the report's conclusions and recom-mendations, are available online at http://shr.aaas.org/guatemala/ceh/mds/spanish.

And the Catholic Church truth commission report: Human Rights Office of the Archdiocese of Guatemala, *Guatemala: Never Again!* Proyecto Interdiocesano de Recuperación de la Memoria Histórica (REMHI), *Guatemala: Nunca Más* (Guatemala City: Oficina de Derechos Humanos del Arzobispado de Guatemala, 1998).

See also the following:

Adams, Richard Newbold. *Crucifixion by Power: Essays on Guatemalan National Social Structure, 1944-1966.* Austin, 1970.

Adams, Richard N,. Santiago Bastos, *Las relaciones étnicas en Guatemala, 1944–2000,* Antigua Guatemala, 2003.

Aguilera Peralta, Gabriel. *Dialéctica del terror en Guatemala.* San Jose, Costa Rica, 1981.

Albizures, Miguel Angel, *Tiempo de sudor y lucha.* Mexico City, 1987.

Arias, Arturo, ed., *The Rigoberta Menchú Controversy.* Minneapolis, 2001.

Ball, Patrick, Paul Kobrak and Herbert Spirer. *State Violence in Guatemala. 1960-1996: A Quantitative Reflection.* Washington DC, 1999.

Bizarro Ujpán, Ignacio. *Campesino: The Diary of a Guatemalan Indian.* Translated and edited by James D. Sexton. Tucson, 1985.

Black, George. *Garrison Guatemala.* New York, 1984.

Black, George, with Norma Stoltz Chinchill and Milton Jamail. *Garrison Guatemala.* New York, 1984.

Brintnall, Douglas E. *Revolt Against the Dead: The Modernization of a Mayan Community in the Highlands of Guatemala.* New York, 1979.

Cardoza y Aragón, Luis. *La revolución Guatemalteca.* Guatemala City, 1994 [1955].

Carlsen, Robert S. *The War for the Heart and Soul of a Highland Maya Town.* Austin: University of Texas Press, 1997.

Carmack, Robert, ed. *Harvest of Violence: The Maya Indians and the Guatemalan Crisis,* Norman, OK, 1988.

Colom, Yolanda. *Mujeres en la alborada.* Guatemala City, 1998.

Cullather, Nick. *Secret History: The CIA's Classified Account of Its Operations in Guatemala. 1952–1954*. Stanford, 1999.

Davis, Sheldon, and Julie Hodson, *Witness to Political Violence in Guatemala*. Boston, 1982.

Falla, Ricardo. *Quiché rebelde: Religious Conversion, Politics, and Ethnic Identity in Guatemala*. Translated by Phillip Berryman. Austin, 2001 [1978].

———. *Massacres in the Jungle: Ixcán, Guatemala, 1975–1982*. Translated by Julia Howland. Boulder, 1994.

Figueroa Ibarra, Carlos. *El proletariado rural en el agro*. San Jose, Costa Rica, 1979.

———. *El recurso del miedo: ensayo sobre el estado y el terror en Guatemala*. San José, Costa Rica, 1991.

Garrard-Burnett, Virginia. *Protestantism in Guatemala: Living in the New Jerusalem*. Austin, 1998.

Garrard-Burnett, Virginia. *Terror in the Land of the Holy Spirit: Guatemala Under General Efraín Ríos Montt, 1982–1983*. Oxford, 2009.

Goldman, Francisco. *The Art of Political Murder: Who Killed the Bishop?* New York, 2007.

Gleijeses, Piero. *Shattered Hope: The Guatemalan Revolution and the United States, 1944–1954*. Princeton, 1991.

Handy, Jim, *Revolution in the Countryside: Rural Conflict and Agrarian Reform in Guatemala. 1944-1954*. Chapel Hill, 1994.

Immerman, Richard. *The CIA in Guatemala: The Foreign Policy of Intervention*. Austin, 1982.

Kobrak, Paul. *Organizing and Repression in the University of San Carlos, Guatemala, 1944 to 1996*. Washington, DC, 1999.

Manz, Beatriz. *Paradise in Ashes: A Guatemalan Journey of Courage, Terror and Hope*. Berkeley, 2004.

———. *Refugees of a Hidden War: The Aftermath of Counterinsurgency in Guatemala*. Albany, 1988.

Montejo, Victor. *Testimony: Death of a Guatemalan Village*. Translated by Victor Perera. Willimantic, CT, 1987.

McClintock, Michael. *The American Connection: State Terror and Popular Resistance in Guatemala*. London, 1985.

Melville, Thomas, and Marjorie Melville. *Tierra y poder en Guatemala*. San José, Costa Rica, 1975.

Melville, Thomas. *Through a Glass Darkly: The US Holocaust in Central America*. Philadelphia, 2005.

Murga Armas, Jorge. *Iglesia catolica, movimiento indigena y lucha revolucionaria*. Santiago Atitlán, Guatemala, 2006.

Nelson, Diane M., *A Finger in the Wound: Body Politics in Quincentennial Guatemala*. Berkeley, 1999.

Perera, Victor. *Unfinished Conquest: The Guatemalan Tragedy*. Berkeley, 1995.

Plant, Roger. *Guatemala: Unnatural Disaster*. London, 1978.

Ramírez, Chiqui. *Guerra de los 36 años: Vista con ojos de mujer de izquierda*. Guatemala City, 2000.

Renato Barillas, Byron, Carlos Alberto Enríquez Prado, Luis Pedro Taracena Arriola. *Tres décadas, dos generaciones: el movimiento estudiantil universitario, una perspectiva desde sus protagonistas.* Guatemala City, 2000.

Salvadó, Luis Raúl, and Julia González. *La ciudad y los desplazados por la violencia.* Guatemala City, 1997.

Saxon, Dan. *To Save Her Life: Disappearance, Deliverance, and the United States in Guatemala.* Berkeley, 2007.

Schirmer, Jennifer. *The Guatemalan Military Project: A Violence Called Democracy.* Philadelphia, 1998.

Schlesinger, Stephen and Stephen Kinzer. *Bitter Fruit: The Untold Story of the American Coup in Guatemala.* New York: Doubleday, 1982.

Simon, Jean-Marie. *Guatemala: Eternal Spring, Eternal Tyranny.* New York, 1987.

Streeter, Stephen. *Managing the Counterrevolution: The United States and Guatemala. 1954–1961.* Athens, OH, 2000.

Taracena Arriola, Arturo, *Etnicidad, estado y nación en Guatemala.* 2 Volumes, Antigua, Guatemala, 2002.

Toriello Garrido, Guillermo. *La batalla de Guatemala.* Guatemala City, 1997 [1955].

———. *Guatemala: Más de 20 años de traición, 1954–1979.* Guatemala City, 1979.

Torres Rivas, Edelberto. *Interpretación del desarrollo social centroamericano.* San Jose, Costa Rica, 1977.

Van Den Berghe, Pierre L., and Benjamin N. Colby. *Ixil Country: A Plural Society in Highland Guatemala.* Berkekey, 1969.

Velásquez Nimatuj, Irma Alicia. *Pueblos indígenas, Estado y Lucha por tierra en Guatemala: Estrategias de sobrevivencia y negociación ante la desigualdad globalizada.* Guatemala City, 2008.

Wilson, Richard. *Maya Resurgence in Guatemala: Q'eqchi' Experiences.* Norman, OK, 1995.

Wilkinson, Daniel, *Silence on the Mountain: Stories of Terror, Betrayal, and Forgetting in Guatamala.* New York, 2002.

Index